D1461424

*Select Works of*
# ROBERT BURNS

LIBRARY
ISLINGTON SIXTH FORM CENTRE
ANNETTE ROAD
LONDON N7 6EX

City and Islington College

SA011884

*Select Works of*

# ROBERT BURNS

VERSE, EXPLANATION AND GLOSSARY

George Scott Wilkie

NEIL WILSON PUBLISHING LIMITED · GLASGOW

LIBRARY
ISLINGTON SIXTH FORM CENTRE
ANNETTE ROAD
LONDON N7 6EX

To my brother Robert, with many thanks
for his help and encouragement.

First published by
Neil Wilson Publishing
303a The Pentagon Centre
36 Washington Street
GLASGOW
G3 8AZ
Tel: 0141-221-1117
Fax: 0141-221-5363
E-mail: nwp@cqm.co.uk
http://www.nwp.co.uk/

All text excluding the original works of Robert Burns
© George Scott Wilkie, 1999

The author has established his moral right to
be identified as the author of this work.

A catalogue record for this book is available
from the British Library.

821.6 BUR

ISBN 1-897784-74-0
Typeset in Jenson
Designed by Mark Blackadder
Printed by WSOY, Finland

# Contents

# Introduction

Many, many words have been written on the life and works of Robert Burns since his death in 1796 at the age of 37. Many of these words have been written by scholars who have researched their treatises with great diligence. Why, then, should anyone else consider it necessary to add to what has already been written in dedication to, and in interpretation of, the words of the Bard?

My reasons are quite simple. There are countless numbers of people throughout the world who are proud of their Scottish ancestry, and who are happy to attend the many traditional Burns Suppers held in honour of the Bard each year, but many of these people struggle to understand a great number of his beautiful poems and songs which were written in the Scots tongue. Millions of people worldwide will join hands as one year passes into the next and mouth the words of Auld Lang Syne without having the faintest notion of the meaning of the words, or indeed, of who penned them.

Many people will harbour the notion that Burns was a simple country ploughman who wrote strange poems about mice and haggis, and who was a bit of a womaniser to boot. But let there be no mistake, Robert Burns was a genius and it is my hope that, by reading some of his verse, they will realise that Burns was anything but a simple ploughman. Burns was educated to a standard that would make many of today's school leavers blush with shame; many of his poems were deeply meaningful, revealing him to be both a lover of womankind, and a staunch advocate of their rights, a man who truly loved nature and who abhorred cruelty, who could see through false piety as though through glass, and who had the amazing ability to use his pen as a sword to destroy his enemies.

It is primarily with these people in mind that I decided to compile some of the Bard's better known works along with several which are not so well known. Among this selection of poems and songs are several which require no explanation whatsoever, as they are written in a style which is totally understandable to any English speaker.

Finally, I must stress that my interpretation of the Bard's works is purely how I, as an individual see them, and is not the result of long academic research.

*George Scott Wilkie*
HEMINGFORD GREY, AUGUST 1999

# Index of First Lines

# To a Mouse

ON TURNING UP THE NEST OF A FIELDMOUSE
WITH HIS PLOUGH, NOVEMBER, 1785

Surely one of the finest poems written by Burns, containing some of the most famous and memorable lines ever written by a poet, yet, to this day, not really understood by the mass of English-speaking poetry lovers, for no other reason than that the dialect causes it to be read as though in a foreign language.

All readers of Burns know of the 'Wee sleekit, cow'rin', tim'rous beastie', but not many understand the sadness and despair contained within the lines of this poem. What was the Bard really saying when he was inspired after turning up a fieldmouse in her nest one day while out ploughing?

Wee sleekit, cow'rin', tim'rous beastie,
Oh, what a panic's in thy breastie!
Thou need na start awa' sae hasty
Wi' bickerin' brattle!
I wad be laith to rin an' chase thee,
Wi' murdering pattle!

The poet is doing his utmost to assure this terrified little creature that he has no intention of causing it any harm
*bickerin' brattle* = scurry, run; *laith* = loath; *pattle* = a small spade for cleaning a plough

I'm truly sorry man's dominion
Has broken Nature's social union,
An' justifies that ill opinion
Which makes thee startle
At me, thy poor, earth-born companion,
An' fellow mortal!

He then goes on to apologise to the mouse for the behaviour of mankind. This requires neither translation nor interpretation.
Listen to what he is saying, and you will be well on your way to understanding what made Burns such a greatly loved man. Note how he equates himself with the mouse in life's great plan.

I doubt na, whyles, but though may thieve;
What then? poor beastie, thou maun live!
A daimen icker in a thrave 's a sma' request
I'll get a blessin' wi' the lave
An' never miss't!

He tells the mouse that he
realizes its need to steal the odd ear
of corn, and he does not mind.
He'll get by with the remainder
and never miss it.
*daimen* = occasional; *icker* = an ear
of corn; *thrave* = twenty-four
sheaves; *lave* = remainder

Thy wee-bit housie, too, in ruin!
Its silly wa's the win's are strewin'!
An' naething, now, to big a new ane
O' foggage green!
An' bleak December wind's ensuin',
Baith snell an' keen!

Dismay at the enormity of the
problems he has brought on the
mouse causes him to reflect on what
he has done – destroyed her home
at a time when it is impossible to
rebuild. There is no grass to build a
new home and the December
winds are cold and sharp. Her
preparations for winter are gone!
*big* = build; *foggage* = moss;
*baith* = both

Thou saw the fields laid bare an' waste
An' weary winter comin' fast,
An' cozie here, beneath the blast,
Thou thought to dwell,
Till crash! the cruel coulter past
Out thro' thy cell

Where the mouse had thought that
she was prepared for winter
in her comfortable little nest in the
ground, now she is faced
with trying to survive in a most
unfriendly climate, with little or
no hope in sight.
*cosie* = comfortable; *coulter* = iron
cutter in front of a ploughshare

That wee bit heap o' leaves an' stibble
Hast cost thee monie a weary nibble!
Now thou's turn'd out, for a' thy trouble
But house or hald,
To thole the winter's sleety dribble,
An' cranreuch cauld!

It seems probable that here the poet is really comparing his own hard times with that of the mouse – a life of harsh struggle, with little or no reward at the end.

*monie* = many; *thole* = to endure; *dribble* = drizzle; *cranreuch* = hoar-frost; *cauld* = cold

But Mousie, thou art no' thy lane,
In proving foresight may be vain;
The best-laid schemes o' mice and men
Gang aft agley
An' lea'e us nought but grief an pain
For promis'd joy!

How many times have people glibly trotted out, 'The best laid schemes' without realising that they were quoting from Burns? The sadness, the despair, the insight contained within this verse are truly remarkable and deeply moving

*no' thy lane* = not alone;
*Gang aft agley* = often go awry

Still, thou art blest', compar'd wi' me!
The present only toucheth thee;
But och! I backward cast my e'e
On prospects drear!
An' forward, tho' I canna see,
I guess an' fear

This final verse reveals the absolute despondency that Burns was feeling at this stage in his life. Not at all what one might expect from a young man of twenty-six, supposedly so popular with the lassies, and with his whole life ahead of him, but nevertheless expressing sentiments with which many of us today can easily relate.

# The Wounded Hare

Once again we hear Burns tell of his sympathy towards the plight of a wild creature. In this instance he recalls hearing a shot while out working in the fields and his anger when, shortly afterwards, he sees a badly injured hare limp by. One can imagine his tears of outrage over such an act of violence and destruction. The meaning of each verse is abundantly clear, therefore I shall not elaborate further.

Inhuman man! curse on thy barb'rous art,
And blasted by thy murder-aiming eye;
May never pity soothe thee with a sigh
Nor never pleasure glad thy cruel heart.

Go live, poor wanderer of the wood and field,
The bitter little that of life remains!
No more the thickening brakes and verdant plains
To thee shall home, or food, or pastime yield.

Seek mangled wretch, some place of wonted rest,
No more of rest, but now thy dying bed!
The sheltering rushes whistling o'er they head,
The cold earth with thy bloody bosom prest.

Oft as by winding Nith I, musing, wait
The sober eve, or hail the cheerful dawn,
I'll miss thee sporting o'er the dewy lawn,
And curse the ruffian's aim, and mourn thy hapless fate.

# The Banks O' Doon

More commonly known as 'Ye Banks and Braes' this sad, wistful song typifies the elegance and beauty of Burn's words when writing of love. He was never more wistful than when he was saying goodbye to one of his many loves, or when he was describing the misfortunes of someone else's love life.

In this case, his tale is of a young lady who has been betrayed by her lover.

Ye banks and braes o' bonie Doon    *bonie* = beautiful
How can ye bloom sae fresh and fair?
How can ye chant, ye little birds,
And I sae weary fu' of care
Thou'll break my heart, thou warbling bird
That wantons thro' the flowering thorn:    *wantons* = to move freely
Thou minds me o' departed joys,
Departed – never to return!

Aft hae I rov'd by bonie Doon,
To see the rose and woodbine twine,
And ilka bird sang o' its love
And fondly sae did I o' mine
Wi' lightsome heart I pu'd a rose,
Fu' sweet upon its thorny tree,
And my fause lover staw my rose,
But ah! He left the thorn wi' me.

The final two lines of this verse tell how the girl's lover stole her rose and left her with nothing but the thorn. Probably, this is a euphemism and she was left with rather more than a broken heart – a not uncommon situation, even in the days of Burns.
*pu'd* = pulled; *fause* = false

# The Rights of Woman

It is an indisputable fact that Robert Burns was a lover of women. His many documented affairs have earned him the reputation of being a true rake and opportunist who would happily seduce any female who fell into his arms, and it is certainly difficult to deny this reputation. However, it must also be said that there is little evidence that those with whom he had his many relationships were other than willing participants.

On the other hand there is another side to the Bard that is not so generally recognised and that many would scorn as being ridiculous. The simple fact is that Burns had enormous respect for women and womanhood and was actually a strong supporter of the feminist movement. Consider, if you will, that it was not until the early 1900s that women in the British Isles began to be taken seriously as people with intelligence, as opposed to being merely domestic drudges, then read these words written by Burns in 1792.

While Europe's eye is fix'd on mighty things,
The fate of empires and the fall of kings;
While quacks of State must each produce his plan,     *quacks* = mere talking pretenders
And even children lisp the Rights of Man;
Amid this mighty fuss, just let me mention,
The Rights of Woman merit some attention.

First, in the sexes' intermix'd connection,
One sacred Right of Woman is Protection:
The tender flower that lifts its head elate,     *elate* = proudly
Helpless must fall before the blasts of fate,
Sunk on the earth, defac'd its lovely form,
Unless your shelter ward th' impending storm.

Our second Right – but needless here is caution –
To keep that right inviolate's the fashion;
Each man of sense has it so full before him,
He'd die before he'd wrong it – 'tis Decorum!
There was, indeed, in far less polish'd days,
A time, when rough rude Man had naughty ways;
Would swagger, swear, get drunk, kick up a riot,
Nay, even thus invade a lady's quiet!
Now, thank our stars! These gothic times are fled;    *gothic* = barbarous
Now, well-bred men – and you are well-bred –
Most justly think (and we are much the gainers)    *gainers* = winners
Such conduct neither spirit, wit nor manners


For Right the third, our last, our best, our dearest:
That right to fluttering female hearts the nearest,
Which even the Rights of Kings, in low prostration,
Most humbly own – tis dear, dear Admiration!
In that blest sphere alone we live and move;    *blest* = blessed
There taste that life of life – Immortal Love.
Smiles, glances, sighs, tears, fits, flirtations, airs –
'Gainst such an host what flinty savage dares?    *'Gainst* = against; *flinty* = cruel
When aweful Beauty joins with all her charms,
Who is so rash as rise in rebel arms?
But truce with kings and truce with constitutions,
With bloody armaments and revolutions;
Let Majesty your first attention summon
*Ah! ça ira!* THE MAJESTY OF WOMEN    *ça ira* = it will be
                                                (French revolutionary song)

# Beware O' Bonie Ann

This poem was dedicated to a young lady from Edinburgh, named Ann Masterton. Ann's father was a schoolmaster and composer and was a friend of Robert Burns.

It is certainly a poem which any young lass would feel flattered to have written in her honour but as we read the various tributes which Burns has composed on behalf of the many other young ladies who have caught his eye, we must question just how much poetic licence the Bard allowed himself – or was 18th century Scotland really awash with flawless beauties?

Ye gallants bright, I rede you right.
Beware o' bonie Ann!
Her comely face sae fu' o' grace,
Your heart she will trepan
Her een sae bright, like stars at night,
Her skin is like the swan;
Sae jimply lac'd her genty waist,
That sweetly ye might span.

*gallants* = splendid men; *rede* = advised; *bonie* = beautiful; *comely* = pleasing; *sae fu' o'* = so full of; *trepan* = snare; *een* = eyes; *jimpy lac'd* = neatly corseted; *genty* = slender

Youth, Grace, and Love, attendant move,
And Pleasure leads the van;
In a' their charms, and conquering arms,
They wait on bonie Ann
The captive bands may chain the hands,
But Love enslaves the man;
Ye gallants braw, I rede you a',
Beware o' bonie Ann!

*van* = those who lead the way

*a'* = all

# Afton Water

This is a particularly lovely piece which is always a great favourite when sung at any Burns gathering. It refers to the River Afton, a small river, the beauty of which obviously greatly enchanted the Bard.

Flow gently, sweet Afton, among thy green braes!   *braes* = banks
Flow gently, I'll sing thee a song in thy praise!
My Mary's asleep by thy murmuring stream –
Flow gently, sweet Afton, disturb not her dream!

Thou stock-dove whose echo                    *stock-dove* = a dove like a small
    resounds thro' the glen               wood-pigeon;
Ye wild whistling blackbirds
    in yon thorny den,                 *yon* = yonder
Thou green-crested lapwing, thy screaming forbear,
I charge you, disturb not my slumbering Fair!

How lofty, sweet Afton,
    thy neighbouring hills,
Far mark'd with the courses of clear, winding rills!   *rills* = small brooks
There daily I wander, as noon rises high,
My flocks and my Mary's sweet cot in my eye    *cot* = cottage

How pleasant thy banks
    and green valleys below,
Where wild in the woodlands
    the primroses blow;
There oft, as mild ev'ning weeps over the lea,
The sweet-scented birk shades my Mary and me.   *birk* = birch

Thy crystal stream, Afton, how lovely it glides,
And winds by the cot where my Mary resides!
How wanton thy waters her snowy feet lave,　　　　*wanton* = luxurious; *lave* = wash
As, gathering sweet flowerets,　　　　　　　　　*flowerets* = little flowers
　　　she stems thy clear wave!　　　　　　　　*stems* = checks


Flow gently, sweet Afton,
　　　among thy green braes,
Flow gently, sweet river, the theme of my lays!　　*lays* = short narrative poems
My Mary's asleep by thy murmuring stream –
Flow gently, sweet Afton, disturb not her dream!

# How Cruel are the Parents

Burns' label as a womanising scoundrel must again be questioned in light of the following lines where he reveals his sympathy towards the unfair treatment of the women of that time, and in particular where the forcing of daughters into arranged marriages where the only consideration was money and where the happiness of the lass was never given serious thought.

There is little doubt but that Burns was a womaniser, but could it be that he was also a visionary who had an extraordinary insight into the plight of women?

How cruel are the parents
Who riches only prize,
And to the wealthy booby,          *booby* = a stupid fellow
Poor Woman sacrifice.
Meanwhile the hapless daughter
Has but a choice of strife;
To shun a tyrant father's hate,
Become a wretched wife.

The ravening hawk pursuing,          The representation of man by the
The trembling dove thus flies,       hawk and woman by the dove is
To shun impelling ruin               particularly sensitive and
Awhile her pinions tries;            thought-provoking.
Till, of escape despairing,
No shelter or retreat,
She trusts the ruthless falconer,
And drops beneath his feet.

# To the Memory of the Unfortunate Miss Burns

Burns was constantly at war with both the church and the law over what he considered to be their tyranny and hypocrisy. This poem was dedicated to a celebrated Edinburgh prostitute whose activities had so offended the City Fathers of Edinburgh that they had banished the unfortunate lady to a nearby village where she died within three years of her expulsion.

The lady's name was Margaret Burns and although we know that the poet and Miss Burns were not related by blood, we know nothing of his relationship with the lady herself. Suffice to say that he knew her well enough to write these few lines in her memory.

By this time, Burns was himself a celebrity and was a favourite in the drawing rooms of the very people he had held in such contempt in his earlier years. This poem is written with little dialect, therefore it requires no words of explanation but it does indicate once again the Bard's ability to produce verse which is as appropriate in today's society as it was some two hundred years ago.


Like to a fading flower in May,
Which gardener cannot save,
So beauty must, sometime, decay
And drop into the grave.


Fair Burns, for long the talk and toast
Of many a gaudy beau,
That beauty has forever lost
That made each bosom glow.

Think fellow sisters on her fate!
Think, think how short her days!
Oh! think and e'er it be too late,
Turn from your evil ways.


Beneath this cold, green sod lies dead    *Edina* = Edinburgh
That once bewitching dame
That fired Edina's lustful sons,
And quenched their glowing flame.

# To a Louse

ON SEEING ONE UPON A LADY'S BONNET AT CHURCH

Here we have one of the Bard's masterpieces, illustrating just how easy it is to have the totally incorrect impression of how we see and are seen by our fellow mortals.

The tale is of Burns sitting in church and noticing a louse crawling on the hat of the lady sitting in front of him and he suggests that this is entirely inappropriate and that it would be more seemly if the creature was on one who was poorer and even older.

The first two lines of the final verse are known throughout the world. The approximate translation is, 'Would that some power could give us the gift to see ourselves as we are seen by others'.

The use of the vernacular calls for a more extensive glossary than in many of the other poems in this book.

Ha! Whare ye gaun, ye crowlin' ferlie?
Your impudence protects you sairlie;
I canna say but ye strunt rarely,
Owre gauze and lace;
Tho', faith I fair, ye dine but sparely
On sic a place

When he first notices the louse, he marvels at its nerve to roam over this fine lady.
*Whare ye gaun* = where are you going; *crawlin' ferlie* = crawling marvel; *sairly* = sorely; *ow're* = over; *sic* = such

Ye ugly creepin blastit wonner.
Detested, shunn'd by saunt an' sinner,
How daur ye set your fit upon her –
Sae fine a lady!
Gae somewhere else and seek your dinner,
On some poor body.

Now he suggests that it is quite wrong for it to be on such a fine lady, and it should find some poor person on which to seek its meal.
*blastit wonner* = worthless wonder; *fit* = foot; *sae* = so

Swith! in some beggar's hauffet squattle,
There ye may creep, and sprawl and sprattle,
Wi' ither kindred, jumpin cattle;
In shoals and nations;
Whaur horn nor bane ne'er daur unsettle
Your thick plantations.

He tells the louse that it would be much more at home with a beggar, sharing that space with its peers in the parasite world, where there was no chance of being routed out by a comb.

*swith* = quick; *hauffet* = sideburns; *squattle* = squat; *sprattle* = scramble; *ither* = other; *horn nor bane* = a comb made of horn or bone

Now haud you there!, ye're out o' sight,
Below the fatt'rils, snug an' tight,
Na, faith ye yet! ye'll no' be right
'Till ye've got on it –
The vera tapmost tow'rin height
O' Miss's bonnet.

Now hold on! The creature has disappeared and it is not going to be content until it is right on top of the lady's hat.

*haud ye there* = wait; *fatt'rels* = ribbon ends; *vera* = very; *tow'rin* = towering

My sooth! right bauld ye set your nose out,
As plump an' grey as onie grozet;
O for some rank, mercurial rozet,
Or fell, red smeddum,
I'd gie you sic a hearty dose o't,
Wad dress your droddum!

Here he sees that the louse is quite plump, and is as grey as a gooseberry and he wishes he had some insect repellent to use on it.

*bauld* = bold; *grozet* = gooseberry; *rozet* = rosin; *fell, red smeddum* = biting red powder; *o't* = of it; *wad* = would; *dress your droddum* = hurt you in the breeches

I wad na been surpris'd to spy
You on an auld wife's flannen toy;
Or aiblins some bit duddie boy,
On's wyliecoat;
But Miss's fine Lunardi! fie!
How daur ye do't?

He would expect the creature on an old woman's flannel cap, or on a lad's ragged vest – but not on a fine Lunardi* bonnet!

*wad na been* = would not have been; *auld wife's flannen toy* = an old woman's flannel cap with side flaps; *aiblins* = perhaps; *duddie* = ragged; *wyliecoat* = a flannel vest; *daur* = dare

O, Jenny, dinna toss your head,
An' set your beauties a' abroad!
Ye little ken what cursed speed
The blastie's makin!
Thae winks an' finger-ends, I dread;
Are notice takin'!

He now makes a silent plea that the lady does not shake her head and spread out her hair as she is totally unaware of what Burns is watching with such fascination.

*dinna* = do not; *yer* = your; *set your beauties a' abroad* = toss your curls; *ken* = know; *blastie* = ugly little creature

O wad some Pow'r the giftie gie us
To see oursels as ithers see us!
It wad frae monie a blunder free us,
An' foolish notion;
What airs in dress an' gait wad lea'e us,
And ev'n devotion!

Finally, the poet leads us to consider ourselves – are we really all that we think we are? Would we not stop making foolish comments about others if we understood ourselves? Food for thought!

*wad* = would; *monie* = many; *lea'e* = leave

* Lunardi bonnets were the height of fashion for ladies at that time. The design was inspired by a balloonist of that name who had made several flights over Scotland.

# The Toad Eater

Four lines which once again display the bard's utter contempt of the *nouveaux riches*, or at least those who were inclined to boast of their wealth and social standing.

This short tirade was directed at one young man in particular who had made a great deal of money through speculation and who, although born of low rank, considered himself to be in the higher echelons of society.

What of earls with whom you have supt,          *supt* = dined
And of dukes that you dined with yestreen?   *yestreen* = yesterday evening
Lord! A louse, Sir, is still but a louse,
Though it crawl on the curls of a queen.

# Holy Willie's Prayer

The church, or the Kirk as it is known in Scotland, was obviously a source for much of Burns' verse. Holy Willie's Prayer is a classic example of how he could see through hypocrisy as if he was looking through glass.

This time his target was an elder (an office-bearer in the Presbyterian Church) of Mauchline Parish, an old bachelor who, although prone to having sexual encounters with certain ladies of the Parish, still considered himself to be far superior to the other lesser mortals who attended the Kirk, and who earnestly believed that the Good Lord should send them all to Hell while, of course, he and his kin should go straight to Heaven.

Should you ever have an opportunity to listen to this poem being told by a true exponent of Burns, then grasp the opportunity – it will be a delight to be savoured for a long, long time.

O Thou, wha in the heavens does dwell,
Wha, as it pleases best Thysel',
Sends ane to Heaven, an' ten to Hell.
A' for Thy glory,
And no' for onie guid or ill
They've done afore Thee!

In the first three verses, Holy Willie is concentrating on ingratiating himself with the Lord, by pointing out just how great and mighty He is.

*ane* = one; *onie guid* = any good

I bless and praise Thy matchless might,
When thousands Thou hast left in night,
That I am here before Thy sight,
For gifts an' grace
A burning an' a shining light
To a' this place.

What was I, or my generation
That I should get sic exaltation?
I, wha deserve most just damnation
For broken laws,
Sax thousand years ere my creation,
Thro' Adam's cause!

*sic* = such
*wha* = who

*sax* = six; *ere* = before

When from my mither's womb I fell,
Thou might hae plung'd me deep in Hell,
To gnash my gooms, and weep and wail
In burning lakes
Where damned devils roar and yell,
Chain'd to their stakes.

The next two verses show us Willie at his best as a groveller but one whose opinion of his own standing knows no bounds.
*mither* = mother

Yet I am here, a chosen sample,
To show Thy grace is great and ample;
I'm here a pillar o' Thy temple,
Strong as a rock,
A guide, a buckler, and example,
To a' Thy flock!

*buckler* = a shield

But yet, O Lord, confess I must
At times I'm fash'd wi' fleshly lust;
An' sometimes, too, wi' wardly trust,
Vile self gets in;
But Thou remembers we are dust
Defil'd wi' sin.

Next, he confesses to his sexual transgressions, but they were all mistakes and not really his fault, because, as he reminds the Lord, we are only made of dust and are susceptible to sin.
*fash'd* = troubled

O Lord! Yestreen, Thou kens, wi' Meg –
Thy pardon I sincerely beg,
O, may't ne'er be a living plague
To my dishonour!
An' I'll ne'er lift a lawless leg
Again upon her.

*Yestreen* = last night; *Thou kens,*
*wi' Meg* = You know, with Meg

Besides I farther maun avow –
Wi' Leezie's lass, three times I trow –
But, Lord, that Friday I was fou
When I cam near her,
Or else, Thou kens, Thy servant true
Wad ne'er hae steered her.

In fact, it had only happened with
Lizzie's daughter because he
had too much to drink, otherwise
he would never have touched her.
*maun avow* = must say;
*trow* = believe; *fou* = drunk;
*steer* = molest

Maybe Thou lets this fleshly thorn
Buffet Thy servant e'en and morn,
Lest he owre proud and high should turn,
That he's sae gifted:
If sae, Thy han' maun e'en be borne,
Until Thou lift it.

Now he starts to wonder if perhaps
the Lord might have given him
this earthly problem to prevent him
from becoming too high and
mighty – even although he is
obviously a very gifted chap.
*e'en and morn* = night and day;
*owre* = over; *Thy han' maun e'en be*
*borne* = the weight of your hand
must always be felt.

Lord, bless Thy chosen in this place,
For here Thou hast a chosen race!
But, God, confound their their stubborn face
An' blast their name,
Wha bring Thy elders to disgrace
An' open shame!

Finally, we discover that the real
purpose of Willie's praying is to
have Holy retribution brought upon
one whom Willie insists is a
disgrace to the community.

Lord, mind Gau'n Hamilton's deserts;
He drinks, an swears, an plays at cartes.
Yet has sae monie takin' arts,
Wi' great an' sma',
Frae God's ain Priest the people's hearts
He steals awa'.

Now he complains to the Lord that
his enemy, Gavin Hamilton, is a
man who drinks and swears and
gambles, but is so popular that he
is turning people away from Kirk.
*cartes* = cards; *so monie takin' arts* = is
so popular; *wi' great an sma* =
with all class of people; *frae* = from;
*ain* = own

An' when we chastened him therefore,
Thou kins how he bred sic a splore,
An' set the warld in a roar
O laughin' at us;
Curse Thou his basket and his store,
Kail an' potatoes!

Here Willie complains that when
he attempted to punish Hamilton,
he caused such an uproar that
everyone finished up by
laughing at Willie.
*sic a splore* = such a fuss;
*kail* = cabbage

Lord, hear my earnest cry and pray'r
Against that Presbyt'ry o' Ayr!
Thy strong right hand, Lord, mak it bare
Upo' their heads!
Lord, visit them, and dinna spare,
For their misdeeds!

While he is at it, Willie decides to
tackle the Lord on another area
giving him problems, the Presbytery
of Ayr. He asks that the Lord
really makes these people suffer for
their wrong-doings.
*hard mak' it bare* = hit them hard;
*dinna spare* = do not let them off

O Lord, my God! That glib-tongu'd Aiken,
My vera heart and flesh are quakin,
To think how we stood sweatin, shakin,
An' pish'd wi' dread,
While he, wi hingin' lip an' snakin',
Held up his head.

The particular culprit is one Robert
Aiken, who had apparently given
Willie a tongue-lashing which had
left him sweating and shaking with
fear and almost wetting himself.

Lord, in Thy day o' vengeance try him!
Lord, visit them wha did employ him!
And pass not in Thy mercy by them
Nor hear their pray'r,
But for Thy people's sake destroy them,
An' dinna spare!

But, Lord, remember me and mine
Wi' mercies temporal and divine,
That I for grace an' gear may shine,
Excelled by nane;
And a' the glory shall be Thine –
Amen, Amen!

Not only does Willie want the Lord to make Aiken suffer, he wants anyone for whom Aiken had ever worked to suffer the same fate, without any mercy.

The final verse is a wonderful example of sanctimonious grovelling, as Willie points out to the Lord, that he, Willie, is such a wonderful person, of such grace, that he and his family should be treated mercifully by the Lord.

*gear* = wealth

# The Slave's Lament

Maya Angelou, the famous black American poet and ardent fan of Robert Burns, expressed her astonishment that Burns had never been to Africa, yet had written this poem. She felt that this must have been written by someone with first-hand knowledge of slavery – someone who had suffered.

Burns, of course, had suffered! Although not a tied slave, he certainly had been a slave to the land and had toiled for too many hours for too little reward. He had a remarkable ability to highlight injustice, equalled by his ability to equate with the lot of the persecuted, so for a man with his remarkable knowledge of the happenings in the word beyond his native shores, penning this work would present no difficulties.


It was in sweet Senegal that my foes did me enthral,        *enthral* = enslave
For the lands of Virginia – ginia, O!
Torn from that lovely shore, and must never see it more,
And alas! I am weary, weary O!


All on that charming coast is no bitter snow or frost,
Like the lands of Virginia – ginia, O
There streams for ever flow, and flowers for ever blow,
And alas! I am weary, weary O!


The burden I must bear, whilst the cruel scourge I fear,
In the lands of Virginia – ginia, O!
And I think on friends most dear, with the bitter, bitter tear,
And alas! I am weary, weary, O!

# Tam O' Shanter

This, without doubt, is one of the most famous poems of Robert Burns. It features both dark humour and nightmarish imagery. It tells the story of a country man, Tam, whose great pleasure in life is imbibing with his friends at the local hostelry and goes on to relate what happens one dreadful night when he comes across Satan, with his warlocks and witches, cavorting in wild revelry in a graveyard. All is going well until Tam gets so carried away with the excitement that the creatures of evil become aware that they are being watched and then all hell breaks loose. Tam O' Shanter is forced to flee for his very life on his old horse, Meg. They must cross the river before they are caught, as the creatures cannot cross running water.

Cutty Sark probably brings to the minds of most readers a well-known brand of Scotch whisky or perhaps the magnificent old tea-clipper which is permanently moored in a dry dock in Greenwich, England. However, Burns introduces the original meaning when he describes the witches dancing in their 'cutty sarks', or underwear (a 'sark' is generally taken to be a shift, or slip, or petticoat, and a 'cutty sark' is a short version of that garment).

*Author's Note*: Should you ever be in the vicinity of Greenwich, go and take a good look at the *Cutty Sark*. There you will see Nannie, the ship's figurehead, dressed in her cutty sark, and yes, that is poor old Meg's tail she is still clutching.

When chapman billies leave the street,
And drouthy neebors, neebors meet;
As market-days are wearing late,
An' folks begin to tak the gate;
While we sit bousing at the nappy,
An' getting fou and unco happy,
We think na on the lang Scots miles,
The mosses, waters, slaps and styles,
That lie between us and our hame,
Whare sits our sulky, sullen dame
Gathering her brows like gathering storm,
Nursing her wrath to keep it warm.

The tale opens in the town of Ayr
on market day. It is getting late,
the pedlars are leaving and
the stallholders are closing but we
find Tam at the local alehouse,
having a good time and not even
thinking about the long journey
home to face an angry wife.
(*Nursing her wrath to keep it warm*:
does that not conjure up a colourful
image? It could apply equally well
today after an extended stay at,
say, the golf club's nineteenth hole.)
*chapman* = pedlar; *billies* = fellows;
*drouthy* = thirsty; *neebors* =
neighbours; *tak the gate* = leave;
*bousing at the nappy* = drinking
strong ale; *fou* = tipsy; *unco* = very;
*slaps* = gaps in fences.

This truth fand honest Tam o' Shanter,
As he frae Ayr ae night did canter:
(Auld Ayr, wham ne'er a town surpasses,
For honest men and bonie lasses)

*fand* = found; *frae* = from

O Tam had'st thou but been sae wise,
As taen thy ain wife Kate's advice!
She tauld thee weel thou was a skellum
A blethering, blustering, drunken blellum;
That frae November till October,
Ae market-day thou was nae sober;
That ilka melder wi' the miller
Thou sat as lang as thou had siller;
That ev'ry naig was ca'd a shoe on
The 'smith and thee gat roarin fou on;
That at the Lord's house, even on Sunday,
Thou drank wi' Kirkton Jean till Monday.
She prophesied that, late or soon,
Thou would be found, deep drown'd in Doon,
Or catch'd wi' warlocks in the mirk
By Alloway's auld haunted kirk

Tam's wife, Kate had told him that he was a good-for-nothing loud-mouth who had never been sober on market day throughout the year. She told him that he would drink as long as he had money – getting drunk with the miller and with the blacksmith – and even on a Sunday, with Kirkton Jean. She warned him that, one of these days, sooner or later, he would be found drowned in the River Doon, or caught in the dark by the demons who lurked around the old haunted church in Alloway.

*tauld* = told; *weel* = weel; *skellum* = a worthless fellow; *bletherin'* = talking nonsense; *blellum* = a babbler; *ilka melder* = every grinding day at the mill; *lang* = long; *siller* = money; *naig* = horse; *ca'd a shoe on* = put on a horseshoe; *gat* = got; *catch'd* = caught; *warlocks* = demons; *mirk* = dark; *auld haunted kirk* = old haunted church

Ah gentle dames, it gars me greet
To think how monie counsels sweet,
How monie lengthen'd, sage advices
The husband frae the wife despises!

But sad to say, Tam, like so many other husbands, paid no attention to his wife's advice.
*gars me greet* = makes me cry; *mony* = many

But to our tale: – Ae market-night
Tam had got planted unco right,
Fast by an ingle, bleezing finely,
Wi' reaming swats, that drank divinely;
And at his elbow, Souter Johnie,
His ancient, trusty, drouthy cronie:
Tam lo'ed him like a very brither,
They had been fou for weeks thegither
The night drave on wi' sangs and clatter;
And ay the ale was growing better
The landlady and Tam grew gracious,
Wi' secret favours, sweet and precious:
The Souter tauld his queerest stories;
The Landlord's laugh was ready chorus:
The storm without might rair and rustle,
Tam did na mind the storm a whistle.

On this particular night Tam was in
his element – he was sitting by
the blazing fire, drinking foaming
pints of beer that tasted better with
each one. By his side was Souter
Johnie, the cobbler. They were old
friends and drinking buddies and
got drunk together every week.
They passed the evening with songs
and small talk and while Tam
flirted with the landlady, Souter
Johnie had the landlord laughing at
his stories. All this time the storm
outside was raging but Tam paid it
no attention.

*planted unco right* = made himself
comfortable; *fast by an ingle* =
beside a fireplace; *bleezing* = blazing;
*reaming swats* = foaming ale;
*souter* = cobbler; *cronie* = comrade;
*lo'ed* = loved; *brither* = brother;
*thegither* = together; *drave on* =
rolled on; *wi' sangs an' clatter* = with
songs and gossip; *ay* = always;
*rair* = roar

Care, mad to see a man sae happy,
E'en drown'd himself amang the nappy
As bees flee hame wi' lades o' treasure,
The minutes wing'd their way wi' pleasure:
Kings may be blest but Tam was glorious,
O'er a' the ills o' life victorious!

Life felt so good for Tam
that night, and as the time flew by,
he was gloriously happy.

*sae* = so; *hame* = home; *lades* = loads

But pleasures are like poppies spread:
You seize the flow'r, its bloom is shed;
Or like the snow falls in the river,
A moment white – then melts for ever;
Or like the borealis race,
That flit ere you can point their place;
Or like the rainbow's lovely form
Evanishing amid the storm.
Nae man can tether time or tide,
The hour approaches Tam maun ride:
That hour, o' night's black arch the key-stane,
That dreary hour Tam mounts his beast in;
An' sic a night he taks the road in,
As ne'er poor sinner was abroad in.

In the first eight lines of this verse,
Burns uses poetry which is
incredibly beautiful and moving to
demonstrate that all good things
must come to an end. It was now
time for Tam to get on his horse
and head for home through the
terrible storm.

*flow'r* = flower; *borealis race* =
the aurora borealis or northern
lights; *flit ere* = move before;
*maun* = must; *key-stane* = key-stone;
*sic* = such; *taks* = takes

The wind blew as 'twad blawn its last;
The rattling showers rose on the blast;
The speedy gleams the darkness swallow'd
Loud, deep, and lang the thunder bellow'd;
That night, a child might understand,
The Deil had business on his hand.

This was the kind of night when
even a child might be aware
that the devil was around.

*'twad blawn* = was blowing

*Deil* = Devil

Weel mounted on his gray mare Meg,
A better never lifted leg,
Tam skelpit on thro' dub and mire,
Despising wind, and rain and fire;
Whiles holding fast his guid blue bonnet,
Whiles crooning o'er an auld Scots sonnet,
Whiles glow'ring round wi' prudent cares,
Lest bogles catch him unawares:
Kirk-Alloway was drawing nigh,
Whare ghaists and houlets nightly cry.

Mounted on his gray mare, Meg, Tam rode on through the storm, holding onto his hat and all the time singing to himself to bolster his courage as he kept glancing about him, in case some goblin would catch him by surprise. But he was getting close to the church at Alloway, where he knew the nights were filled with the cries of ghosts and owls.

*meare* = mare; *skelpit on* = hurried on; *thro' dub and mire* = through puddles and mud; *guid* = good; *bogles* = goblins; *ghaists and houlets* = ghosts and owls

By this time he was cross the ford,
Whare in the snaw the chapman smoor'd;
And past the birks and meikle stane,
Whare drunken Charlie brak's neck-bane;
And thro' the whins, and by the cairn,
Whare hunters fand the murder'd bairn;
And near the thorn, aboon the well,
Whare Mungo's mither hang'd hersel.
Before him Doon pours all his floods;
The doubling storm roars thro' the woods;
The lightnings flash from pole to pole,
Near and more near the thunders roll;
When, glimmering thro' the groaning trees,
Kirk-Alloway seem'd in a bleeze,
Thro' ilka bore the beams were glancing,
And loud resounded mirth and dancing.

Now he was at the scary part of his journey. After he crossed the ford he was in the area where several frightening events had taken place: where a pedlar had smothered in the snow; where drunken Charlie had fallen and broken his neck at the big stone; where some hunters had found the body of a murdered child; where Mungo's mother had hanged herself. And all the time the storm raged on! Tam could see that the church was brightly lit and there was the sound of laughter and dancing.

*whare* = where; *snaw* = snow; *chapman;* = pedlar; *smoor'd* = smothered; *birks* = birche trees; *meikle stane* = big stone; *brak's neck-bane;* = broke his neck; *whins* = gorse; *calm* = a heap of stones; *fand* = found; *bairn* = child; *aboon* = above; *bleeze* = blaze; *thro' ilka bore* = through the gaps in the trees

Inspiring bold John Barleycorn,
What dangers thou canst make us scorn!
Wi' tipenny, we fear nae evil;
Wi' usquabae, we'll face the Devil!
The swats sae reamed in Tammie's noddle,
Fair play, he car'd na deils a boddle.
But Maggie stood, right sair astonish'd,
Till, by the heel and hand admonished,
She ventur'd forward on the light;
And vow! Tam saw an unco sight!

It is amazing the courage that drinking can give. With a few beers we fear no evil and add some whisky and we will take on the Devil himself. And so, Tam, his brain addled by his night of imbibing, didn't give a farthing for what he might come across. But such was not the case with Meg and she had to be given a kick to get her going again. And what a picture they saw!

*John Barleycorn* = malt whisky; *tippenny* = ale; *usquabae* = whisky; *noddle* = head; *he car'd na deils a boddle* = he did not care a farthing for the devils; *sair* = sore; *unco* = strange

Warlocks and witches in a dance:
Nae cotillion, brent new frae France,
But hornpipes, jigs, strathspeys and reels,
Put life and mettle in their heels.
A winnock-bunker in the east,
There sat Auld Nick, in shape o' beast;
A touzie tyke, black, grim and large,
To gie them music was his charge:

The goblins and witches were dancing – not a decorous French cotillion, but wild Scottish reels and strathspeys. And there, in a window-seat in the church, was Satan himself – playing the music for his terrible horde.

*warlocks* = demons; *brent* = brand; *winnock-bunker* = window-seat; *auld Nick* = Satan; *towzie tyke* = unkempt dog; *gie* = give

He screw'd the pipes and gart them skirl,
Till roof and rafters a' did dirl.
Coffins stood round, like open presses,
That shaw'd the dead in their last dresses;
And by some devilish cantraip sleight,
Each in its cauld hand held a light:
By which heroic Tam was able
To note upon the haly table,
A murderer's banes, in gibbet-airns;
Twa span-lang, wee unchristen'd bairns;
A thief new-cutted frae a rape –
Wi' his last gasp his gab did gape;
Five tomahawks, wi' bluid red-rusted;
Five scymitars, wi' murder crusted;
A garter which a babe had strangled;
A knife a father's throat had mangled –
Whom his ain son o'life bereft –
The grey-hairs yet stack to the heft;
Three lawyers' tongues turned inside-out
Wi' lies seamed like a beggar's clout;
Three priests' hearts rotten, black as muck,
Lay stinking, vile in every neuk.
Wi' mair of horrible and awfu'
Which even to name wad be unlawfu'

The scene was horrific. While Satan was making the rafters ring with his pipes, there were coffins standing around, open like cupboards and in each one was a corpse with a candle in its cold hand. On the altar there were some dreadful relics of unspeakable events that had taken place – including hangings and murders.

*gart* = made; *a'* = all; *dirl* = vibrate; *presses* = cupboards; *shaw'd* = showed; *devilish cantraip sleight* = black magic; *cauld han'* = cold hand; *haly table* = altar; *banes* = bones; *gibbet-airns* = gibbet irons; *twa span-lang, wee unchristen'd bairns* = two nine-inch-long unchristened babies; *new-cutted frae a rape* = just cut down from a hangman's noose; *gab did gape* = mouth wide open; *bluid* = blood; *heft* = handle; *clout* = ragged clothes; *muck* = wet filth; *neuk* = nook and cranny; *mair* = more; *awfu'* = awful

As Tammie glowr'd, amaz'd and curious,
The mirth and fun grew fast and furious;
The piper loud and louder blew,
The dancers quick and quicker flew,
They reel'd, they set, they cross'd, they cleekit,
Till ilka carlin swat and reekit,
And coost her duddies to the wark,
And linket at it in her sark!

As Tam stared in fascination, the dancing got even faster and faster until the dancers were soaked in sweat and threw off their clothes and danced only in their petticoats. *glowr'd* = stared; *cleekit* = linked together; *ilka carlin swat and reekit* = every old woman sweated and panted; *coost her duddies on the wark* = cast off her rags; *linket at it in her sark* = danced in her slip

Now Tam, O Tam! Had thae been queans,
A' plump and strapping in their teens!
Their sarks, instead o' creeshie flannen,
Been snaw-white seventeen hunder linen! –
Thir breeks o'mine, my only pair,
That ance were plush, o' guid blue hair,
I wad hae gien them off my hurdies,
For ae blink o' the bonie burdies!
But wither'd beldams, auld and droll,
Rigwoodie hags wad spean a foal,
Louping and flinging on a crummock,
I wonder did na turn thy stomach!

If only they had been young women in clean clothes, then Tam could easily have let his desires get the better of him and shed his trousers. But these wrinkled, ugly old women wearing greasy flannel, who were leaping and capering with their cudgels was almost enough to make Tam throw up. *queans* = young women; *creeshie flannen* = greasy flannel; *snaw-white* = snow-white; *seventeen hunder linen* = fine-gauge linen; *thir breeks* = these trousers; *ance* = once; *I wad hae gien them off my hurdies* = I would have given them off my behind; *bonie burdies* = lovely girls; *beldams* = old hags; *droll* = peculiar; *ringwoodie* = gallows-worthy; *crummock* = cudgel

32

But Tam kent what was what fu' brawlie:
There was ae winsome wench and wawlie,
That night enlisted in the core
Lang after kend on Carrick shore,
(For monie a beast to dead she shot,
An' perish'd monie a bonie boat,
And shook baith meikle corn and bear,
And kept the country-side in fear.)
Her cutty sark, o' Paisley harn,
That while a lassie she had worn
In longitude tho' sorely scanty,
It was her best, and she was vauntie –
Ah! little kend thy reverend grannie,
That sark she coft for her wee Nannie,
Wi' twa pund Scots (twas a' her riches),
Wad ever grac'd a dance of witches!

But Tam had spotted the one who was different, a lively attractive girl who had just joined the corp of witches that night (he was not aware of the evil and the deaths she had wrought).

She was wearing a petticoat that her grandmother had used all her savings to buy for her when she was a little girl and who had never thought that it would ever be worn in a dance of witches. It was really more than a bit short for her, but it was her best and she was rather vain about it.

*kent...fu' brawlie* = knew very well; *winsome wench and wawlie* = a jolly, attractive girl; *core* = corp; *lang after kenn'd* = known long after; *Paisley harn* = a coarse cloth; *vauntie* = vain; *coft* = bought; *twa pounds Scots* = two Scottish pounds

But here my Muse her wing maun cour,
Sic flights are far beyond her power:
To sing how Nannie lap and flang,
(A souple jade she was, and strang)
And how Tam stood like ane bewitch'd,
And thought his very een enrich'd;
Even Satan glowr'd and fidg'd fu' fain,
And hotch'd and blew wi' might and main:
'Till first ae caper, syne anither,
Tam tint his reason a' thegither,
An' roars out, 'Weel done, Cutty-Sark!'
An' in an instant all was dark:
An' scarcely had he Maggie rallied
When out the hellish legion sallied.

This young witch, Nannie, was an incredible dancer and Tam was enthralled just watching her, as was Satan himself who was struggling to keep his music going while leering at the dancer. But Tam forgot where he was and in a moment of lunancy, so carried away was he by the spectacle, that he shouted out, 'Well done Cutty-Sark'.
There was instant darkness and he hardly had time to get Maggie moving when the dreadful band came streaming out of the churchyard, intent on catching this interloper.

*her wing maun cour* = her imagination must be curbed; *lap and flang* = leaped and capered; *souple* = supple; *jade* = an ill-natured woman; *strang* = strong; *ane* = one; *een* = eyes; *fidg'd fu' fain* = fidgeted in excitement; *syne* = then; *tint* = lost

As bees bizz out wi' angry fyke,
When plundering herds assail their byke;
As open pussie's mortal foes,
When pop! She starts before their nose;
As eager runs the market-crowd,
When 'Catch the thief' resounds aloud:
So Maggie runs, the witches follow,
Wi' monie an eldritch skriech an' hollow.

Just like a swarm of angry bees after an intruder disturbs their hive so the creatures of evil came storming after Tam and Maggie, filling the darkness with their frightening screams and screeches.

*bizz* = buzz; *fyke* = fuss; *herds* = shepherds; *byke* = bee-hive; *pussie* = hare; *eldritch skriech and hollow* = unearthly, frightful screams

Ah, Tam! Ah, Tam! Thou'll get thy fairin'
In hell they'll roast thee like a herrin'!
In vain thy Kate awaits thy comin'!
Kate soon will be a woefu' woman!
Now, do thy speedy utmost, Meg,
And win the key-stane of the brig;
There, at them thou thy tail may toss,
A running stream they dare na cross!
But ere the key-stane she could make,
The fient a tail she had to shake;
For Nannie, far before the rest
Hard upon noble Maggie prest,
And flew at Tam w' furious ettle;
But little wist she Maggie's mettle!
Ae spring brought off her master hale,
But left behind her ain gray tail:
The carlin caught her by the rump,
And left poor Maggie scarce a stump.

Tam, what have you done? Now you are going to get your just reward. You will finish up in hell, being roasted like a herring. Kate will never see you again, unless...unless Maggie can get across the bridge before the witches catch up with you, because witches cannot cross running water. Maggie was going well but there was one witch who was away in front of the others – Nannie. She was right at their back and gaining. At the very last moment, Maggie made a surge and brought Tam past the important key-stone of the bridge. But it was not without cost – the evil Nannie had made a desperate grab for Tam but missed and caught the horse's rump, catching her tail which then came off, leaving poor Maggie with only a stump.

*fairin'* = reward; *brig* = bridge; *dare na'* = dare not; *fient* = fiend; *prest* = pressed; *ettle* = intention; *little wist she Maggie's mettle* = little did she know Maggie's spirit; *hale* = whole; *carlin* = shrew; *claught* = clutched

Now, wha this tale o' truth shall read,
Ilk man, and mother's son take heed:
Whene'er to drink you are inclin'd
Or cutty sarks rin in your mind,
Think! ye may buy the joys o'er dear:
Remember Tam o' Shanter's mare.

Now pay attention every man and mother's son who reads this true tale. Any time you think about having a drink or if the thought of a girl in a short petticoat crosses your mind, you may have to pay a high price for these pleasures – remember Tam o' Shanter's mare.

*rin* = run

35

# My Luve is Like a Red, Red Rose

In order to demonstrate the versatility of Robert Burns, I have deliberately placed this, (in my opinion the most beautiful, romantic poem or love song ever written) to follow the rambunctious Tam o'Shanter. 'Tam' has a fast, exciting pace, while this poem is gentle and sentimental. Apparently, experts believe that Burns used an old ballad or possibly a combination of several old ballads, as the basis for this work.

The work is as beautiful today as it was when first composed over two hundred years ago.

O my luve is like a red, red rose.
That's newly sprung in June.                          *sprung* = blossomed
O, my luve is like the melodie
That's sweetly play'd in tune.

As fair art thou, my bonie lass,
So deep in luve am I,
And I will luve thee still, my dear,
Till a' the seas gang dry.                            *till a' the seas gang dry* = until all the seas dry up

Till a' the seas gang dry, my dear,
And the rocks melt wi' the sun!
And I will luve thee still, my dear,
While the sands o' life shall run.

And fare thee weel, my only luve!                     *fare thee weel* = farewell
And fare thee weel, a while!
And I will come again, my luve,
Tho' 'twere ten thousand mile!                        *Tho' 'twere* = although it were

# A Man's a Man for a' That

In this poem, Burns clearly reveals his contempt for rank and title. It was written in 1795, a year before his death, and it gives the impression that by that time he had developed an intense dislike of the aristocracy. Perhaps his rubbing shoulders with Edinburgh's upper-crust helped create his dislike, but we can only surmise.

However, the fact does remain that this poem has attained international recognition among those who believe in the equality of man. The Russians honoured Burns by issuing four commerative stamps of him during the twentieth century and his works continue to be part of the school curriculum in that country.

Unfortunately the hope expressed in the final verse shows little sign of coming to fruition.

Is there for honest poverty
That hings his head, an' a' that?
The coward slave, we pass him by –
We dare be poor for a' that!
For a' that an' a' that,
Our toils obscure an' a' that
The rank is but the guinea's stamp,
The man's the gowd for a' that.

Here Burns is telling us that although a man be poor and a hard worker, he is still a man. Burns has no time for either the servile creature who always hangs his head or for the would-be high and mighty person who bought such power.
*hings* = hangs; *gowd* = gold

What though on hamely fare we dine,
Wear hoddin grey an' an' that?
Gie fools their silks, and knaves their wine
A man's a man for a' that
For a' that an' a' that,
Their tinsel show, an' a' that,
The honest man, tho' e'er sae poor,
Is king o' men for a' that

Just because a man dines on simple food and wears clothes that may not be considered fashionable, it does not make him any less a man than one whose clothes are made of silk and who drinks wine.
*hamely fare* = homely food;
*hoddin grey* = a coarse grey woollen cloth; *gie* = give

Ye see yon birkie ca'd 'a lord',
Wha struts, an stares, an' a' that?
Tho' hundreds worship at his word,
He's but a cuif for a' that.
For a' that, an' a' that.
His ribband, star, an' a' that,
The man o' independent mind,
He looks an' laughs at a' that.

Look at that swaggering fellow who
is called 'a lord' with hundreds of
people listening to his every word –
in actual fact he is nothing but
a fool. A real man just looks at all
the ribbons and stars being worn
and laughs at them.
*birkie* = a strutting swaggering
fellow; *cuif (coof)* = fool;
*ribband* = ribbon

A prince can mak a belted knight,
A marquis, duke an' a' that!
But an honest man's aboon his might –
Guid faith, he mauna fa' that,
For a' that, an' a' that,
Their dignities an' a' that,
The pith o' sense an' pride o' worth,
Are higher rank than a' that

Any man can be given a title by
royalty but that does not make
him any better than an honest man
who has faith in himself. To know
one's worth is value in excess of the
foolish dignity of these people.
*mak* = make; *aboon* = above;
*gude* = good; *mauna* = must not
*fa'* = fall; *pith* = importance

Then let us pray that come it may
(As come it will for a' that)
That Sense and Worth o'er a' the earth,
Shall bear the gree an' a' that
For a' that an' a' that,
It's comin' yet for a' that
That man to man, the world o'er
Shall brithers be for a' that.

However let us pray that one of
those days men will see the
pointlessness of struggle over rank
and power and come to
recognise that all men are equal.
*bear the gree* = win the victory

# For the Sake O' Somebody

These two short verses were not, as we might have come to expect, written by the Bard about a very special young lady; in fact they were written about no less a person than Bonie Prince Charlie

My heart is sair, I dare na tell,
My heart is sair for Somebody;
I could wake a winter night,
For the sake o' Somebody!
Oh-hon! For Somebody!
Oh-hey! For Somebody!
I could range the world around
For the sake o' Somebody.

*sair* = aching; *dare na* = dare not

Ye powers that smile on virtuous love,
O, sweetly smile on Somebody!
Frae ilka danger keep him free,
And send me safe my Somebody!
Oh-hon! for Somebody!
Oh-hey! for Somebody!
I wad do – what wad I not?
For the sake o' Somebody

*Frae ilka* = from every

*wad* = would

# Ae Fond Kiss

It was never my intent, when compiling this book, to delve into the life of the poet, as that task has been performed on many occasions by dedicated writers and researchers who have given us a magnificent insight into Burns. However, I feel that it is important to explain that this particular poem was dedicated to a married lady by the name of Nancy McLehose, with whom Burns had shared a clandestine, although platonic, affair. Burns had written many letters and poems to his darling Nancy, but had disguised the object of his love by addressing them to Clarinda, and signing himself Sylvander. When, in 1792, Nancy left Scotland and sailed for Jamaica to attempt a reconciliation with her husband, Burns was inspired to write this beautiful song.

Ae fond kiss, and then we sever;  *sever* = separate
Ae farewell, and then forever!
Deep in heart-wrung tears I'll pledge thee,
Warring sighs and groans I'll wage thee,  *wage* = pledge
Who shall say that Fortune grieves him,
While the star of hope she leaves him?
Me, nae cheerful twinkle lights me;
Dark, despair around benights me.  *benights* = clouds with disappointment

I'll ne'er blame my partial fancy
Naething could resist my Nancy;  *naething* = nothing
But to see her was to love her;
Love but her, and love for ever;
Had we never lov'd sae kindly  *sae* = so
Had we never lov'd sae blindly,
Never met – or never parted,
We had ne'er been broken-hearted.

Fare-thee-weel, thou first and fairest!     *Fare-thee-weel* = farewell

Fare-thee-weel, thou best and dearest!

Thine be ilka joy and treasure,     *ilka* = every

Peace, Enjoyment, Love, and Pleasure!

Ae fond kiss, and then we sever!

Ae fareweel, alas, for ever!

Deep in heart-wrung tears I'll pledge thee,

Warring sighs and groans I'll wage thee.

# On the Birth of a Posthumous Child

BORN IN PECULIAR CIRCUMSTANCES OF FAMILY DISTRESS

In 1790 a Swiss-born gentleman, named James Henri died suddenly leaving behind a young widow, Susan Dunlop, in an advanced state of pregnancy. The Bard was extremely fond of both Susan and her mother and when Susan gave birth to a son, he wrote the following lines to the boy, sending them to Mrs Dunlop, senior. This poem displays clearly how Burns was able to transfer tragedy into a thing of beauty and he once again reveals his high level of sensitivity and compassion.

Sweet flow'ret, pledge o' meikle love,
And ward o' monie a prayer,
What heart o' stane wad thou na move,
Sae helpless, sweet and fair!

*flow'ret* = litle flower; *pledge o'* = result of; *meikle* = great; *monie* = many; *stane* = stone; *na* = not; *Sae* = so

November hirples o'er the lea,
Chill, on thy lovely form;
And gane, alas! the shelt'ring tree,
Should shield thee frae the storm.

*hirples* = limps; *o'er* = over; *lea* = grass
*gane* = gone

May He who gives the rain to pour,
And wings the blast to blaw,
Protect thee frae the driving show'r
The bitter frost and snaw!

*blast to blaw* = wind to blow
*frae* = from
*snaw* = snow

May He, the friend of Woe and Want,
Who heals life's various stounds,
Protect and guard the mother plant
And heal her cruel wounds!

*stounds* = times of trouble

But late she flourish'd rooted fast,
Fair on the summer morn,
Now feebly bends she in the blast,
Unshelter'd and forlorn


Blest by thy bloom, thy lovely gem,
Unscath'd by ruffian hand!
And from thee many a parent stem             *stem* = branch forth
Arise to deck our land!                      *deck* = grace

# Scots Wha Hae

The verses of this song, guaranteed to make the blood course strongly through the veins of any true Scot, were written by Burns after visiting the field of Bannockburn in 1787. In common with most other Scots who have visited the site throughout the years, he appears to have been overwhelmed by the vision of a free Scotland, fired, no doubt, by the apparent success of the French Revolution which had dominated the news for the past year.

Scots, wha hae wi' Wallace bled,
Scots, wham Bruce has aften led,
Welcome to your gory bed,
Or to victorie!
Now's the day and now's the hour;
See the front o' battle lour;
See approach proud Edward's power
Chains and slaverie!

As the time for battle draws near, Burns visualises Bruce reminding his men that Scots have already shed their blood alongside William Wallace and that he, Bruce, has led them before against the enemy. Today however is win or die – or worse – become a slave of King Edward.
*wha hae* = who have; *wham* = whom; *gory* = bloody; *lour* = threaten

Wha will be a traitor knave?
Wha can fill a coward's grave?
Wha sae base as be a slave?
Let him turn and flee!
Wha for Scotland's King and Law,
Freedom's sword will strongly draw,
Free-man stand, or free-man fa',
Let him follow me!

He asks if any of his men could be traitors or cowards or willing to accept the life of a slave. If so then turn and flee now. But if they are willing to fight for Scotland and their King, then follow him and live or die as free men.
*sae base* = so worthless

By Oppression's woes and pains!
By your Sons in servile chains!
We will drain our dearest veins,
But they *shall* be free!
Lay the proud usurpers low!
Tyrants fall in every foe!
Liberty's in every blow!
Let us do – or die!

To fight the oppressor is to fight for the freedom of their own children. They themselves may die in battle but their children will be free. Every blow struck is a blow for liberty. Fight or die!

# The Dumfries Volunteers

In sharp contrast to the profoundly Scottish sentiments expressed in Scots Wha Hae, here Burns appears to be truly British although this was probably an attempt to satisfy his masters in the Excise. In 1795 there was great speculation that Napoleon was set to invade the British Isles and this led to the formation of the Volunteers Movement, an early version of the Home Guard of the Second World War. Burns was heavily involved in the formation of the Dumfries group and certainly appears to have enjoyed this aspect of his life. One can only wonder what Robert Burns would have made of today's squabbles with Britain's European partners.

Does haughty Gaul invasion threat?
Then let the loons beware, Sir!
There's wooden walls upon our seas,
And volunteers on shore, Sir!
The Nith shall run to Corsincon,
And Criffel sink in Solway,
Ere we permit a foreign foe
On British ground to rally!

He points out that should the French be foolish enough to launch an invasion, they will be confronted by the navy and the ranks of volunteers. The River Nith and the hills of Corsincon and Criffel will have to perform geographical miracles before any enemy of Britain will rally on British soil.

Gaul = France; loons = rascals; wooden walls = ships

O let us not like snarling tykes
In wrangling be divided;
Till, slap! come in an unco loon
And wi' a rung decide it.
Be Britain still to Britain true,
Amang oursels united;
For never but by British hands
Maun British wrangs be righted!

He warns that fighting among ourselves could be fatal, as we are liable to find too late that the enemy has taken over and that they now rule the British with clubs and cudgels. Only by remaining united will the British right the wrongs within Britain.

*tykes* = dogs; *unco* = fearsome; *rung* = cudgel; *amang* = among *maun* = must; *wrangs* = wrongs

The kettle o' the Kirk and State
Perhaps a clout may fail in't!
But deil a foreign tinkler loon
Shall ever ca' a nail in't!
Our fathers' bluid the kettle bought,
And wha wad dare to spoil it!
By heaven, the sacrilegious dog
Shall fuel be to boil it!

There may be differences between Church and State but no foreigner is going to be allowed to interfere. British freedom was bought with the blood of our forefathers so heaven help anyone who attempts to take away that freedom – especially a Frenchman!

*kettle* = boiling pot; *Kirk* = church; *clout* = piece of cloth; *tinkler* = gypsy; *ca'* = drive; *bluid* = blood; *wha wad* = who would

The wretch that wad a tyrant own,
And the wretch his true-sworn brother,
Who would set the mob aboon the throne,
May they be damned together!
Who will not sing 'God save the King',
Shall hang as high's the steeple;
But while we sing 'God save the King,'
We'll ne'er forget the People!

Any despicable person who would help overthrow the King, and who refuses allegiance to the throne, will be hanged. But remember, even as we swear loyalty to our King, we must never overlook the rights of the common man.

*aboon* = above

# Address to a Haggis

No Burns Supper could ever take place without the wonderful ritual of the Address to a Haggis. This recital is usually performed in a very theatrical and flamboyant manner with a great flow of words, totally incomprehensible to the ear of the non-Scot (and truth be told, even to some Scots). It is a truly wonderful poem, full of humour, so let's see if we can find our way through the vernacular and at least make the theme a little more understandable to those who find it so daunting. I believe there is a school of thought which thinks that Burns wrote this poem purely as a piece of fun and never intended it to be taken seriously. No matter! It has become part of the Scottish tradition and will never, ever be forgotten.

Fair fa' your honest, sonsie face,
Great chieftain o' the puddin'-race!
Aboon them a' ye tak your place,
Painch, tripe or thairm;
Weel are ye wordy o' a grace
As lang's my airm.

He begins with a simple statement – a haggis is the greatest of all puddings. Greater than stomach, tripe or guts, and well worth this long grace.
*sonsie* = jolly; *puddin-race* = meat puddings or sausages; *aboon* = above; *painch, tripe or thairm* = animal entrails; weel = well; *wordy* = worthy; *grace* = a prayer; *lang* = long; *airm* = arm

The groaning trencher there ye fill,
Your hurdies like a distant hill,
Your pin wad help to mend a mill
In time o' need
While thro' your pores the dews distil
Like amber bead.

It fills the platter and its buttocks look like a distant hill. Its skewer is large enough to repair a broken-down mill and the succulent moisture oozing from it is as beautiful as amber beads.
*groaning trencher* = laden platter; *hurdies* = hips or buttocks; *pin* = skewer; wad = would

His knife see rustic Labour dight,
An' cut you up wi' ready slight,
Trenching your gushing entrails bright,
Like ony ditch;
And then, O what a glorious sight,
Warm-reekin, rich!

With a skilled hand the server cuts through the skin, which flows open like a ditch as the insides gush forth. But what a glorious sight with its warm, steaming, richness.
*dight* = to clean; *trenching* = cutting open; *ony* = any; *warm-reekin* = warm-smelling

Then, horn for horn, they stretch an' strive,
Deil tak the hindmost, on they drive,
Till a' their weel-swall'd kytes belyve
Are bent like drums;
Then auld Guidman, maist like to rive,
'Bethankit' hums.

Spoonful by spoonful, everyone digs in and the devil takes the slowest eater until everyone is replete. Then the bulging elder of the family leans back and hums his thanks.
*horn* = a spoon;
*weel-swall'd kytes* = full bellies;
*belyve* = eventually; *bent like drums* = tight as drums; *auld* = old;
*maist* = most; *rive* = burst;
'*Bethankit*' = God be thanked

Is there that owre his French *ragout*,
Or *olio* that wad staw a sow,
Or *fricassee* wad make her spew
Wi' perfect sconner,
Looks down wi' sneerin, scornfu' view
On sic a dinner?

Can anyone who has eaten all that fancy French rubbish, so disgusting as to make a pig throw up, dare to look down his nose and sneer at such a dinner?
*owre* = over; *ragout/olio* = savoury dishes of meat and vegetables;
*staw a sow* = stop a pig;
*fricassee* = dish of fowl or rabbit;
*spew* = vomit; *sconner* = disgust; *sic* = such

Poor devil! see him owre his trash,
As feckless as a wither'd rash,
His spindle shank a guid whiplash,
His nieve a nit;
Thro' bluidy flood or field to dash
O how unfit!

Look at that poor devil bent over
the rubbish he is eating. He's
as weak as a withered rush. His legs
are skinny and his fist is no
bigger than a nut. No working in
the fields for him – he's too unfit!
*feckless* = helpless; *spindle shank* =
thin leg; *guid* = good
*nieve* = fist; *nit* = nut

But mark the Rustic, haggis-fed,
The trembling earth resounds his tread,
Clap in his walie nieve a blade,
He'll make it whissle;
An' legs, an' arms an' heads will sned,
Like taps o' thrissle.

But see that labourer fed on haggis.
The earth trembles under his feet
and in his great fist a sword would
whistle through the air lopping
off legs, arms and heads as though
they were no more than the tops of
thistles.
*walie nieve* = large fist; *blade* =
a sword; *whissle* = whistle;
*sned* = lop off; *taps o' thrissle* =
tops of thistles

Ye Pow'rs, wha mak mankind your care,
And dish them out their bill o' fare,
Auld Scotland wants nae skinking ware
That jaups in luggies;
But, if ye wish her gratefu' prayer
Gie her a Haggis!

Mark, you powers that look after
mankind and provide us with our
food, Scotland does not want
watery rubbish splashing about in
dishes. If you want her grateful
thanks – give her a haggis!
*bill o' fare* = menu; *skinking ware* =
watery dish; *jaups* = splashes;
*luggie* = wooden dish with handles;
*gie* = give

# Pretty Peg

Yet another short poem by the Bard, extolling his virtues of a young lady. The sentiment speaks for itself and requires no elaborating on my part.

As I gaed up by yon gate-end
When day was waxin' weary,
Wha did I meet come down the street,
But pretty Peg, my dearie?

*gaed up by yon gate-end* = went up by the end of the street; *waxin'* = beginning; *wha* = who; *dearie* = loved one

Her air sae sweet, and shape complete,
Wi' nae proportion wanting
The Queen of Love did never move
Wi' motion mair enchanting!

*air* = appearance; *sae* = so; *nae* = no; *wanting* = lacking; *mair* = more

Wi' linked hands we took the sands
Down yon winding river;
And oh! that hour and shady bower,
Can I forget it? Never!

# To a Mountain Daisy

The Bard was going through a very unhappy period in his life when he wrote this poem and his deep unhappiness at his situation is abundantly clear in the melancholy tone which he has adopted in its composition.

It would seem that the activity of ploughing allowed him time for deep meditation, for it was on such an occasion that the sigh of a daisy caught his eye and inspired the following words.

Wee, modest, crimson-tipped flow'r,
Thou's met me in an evil hour;
For I maun crush amang the stoure
Thy slender stem:
To spare thee now is past my pow'r
Thou bonie gem.

The ploughman is speaking to the daisy and apologising for its accidental uprooting, but unfortunately, at this stage there is nothing he can do about it.
*maun* = must; *amang the stoure* = among the dust; *stem* = stalk; *thou bonie gem* = you lovely, precious thing

Alas, it's no' thy neebor sweet,
The bonie lark, companion meet,
Bending thee 'mang the dewy weet,
Wi' spreckl'd breast!
When upward-springing, blythe, to greet
The purpling east.

He explains that sadly it was not a friendly lark which was bending the flower's stalk as it sprang upward to meet the sun rising in the east.
*no'* = not; *neebor* = neighbour; *'mang the dewy weet* = among the dewy wet; *spreckled* = speckled; *the purpling east* = the sunrise

Cauld blew the bitter-biting north
Upon thy early humble birth;
Yet cheerfully thou glinted forth
Amid the storm,
Scarce rear'd above the parent-earth
Thy tender form.

Although the bitter north wind was
blowing when it came through
the surface, the daisy had still
appeared bright and cheerful
throughout the storm, even
although it was so small that
its head barely rose above the earth.
*cauld* = cold; *north* = north wind;
*glinted* = gleamed

The flaunting flow'rs our gardens yield,
High shelt'ring woods and wa's maun shield;
But thou, beneath the random bield
O' clod or stane,
Adorns the histie stibble field
Unseen, alane.

Gardens may have beautiful flowers
but they are sheltered by woods
and walls. The daisy had to
survive alone, surrounded by mud
and earth and stone, seldom seen by
anyone.
*wa's* = walls; *maun* = must; *bield o'*
*clod or stane* = shelter of earth or
stone; *histie stibble field* = field of dry
stubble; *alane* = alone

There, in thy scanty mantle clad,
Thy snawie bosom sun-ward spread,
Thou lifts thy unassuming head
In humble guise;
But now the share uptears thy bed,
And low thou lies!

There was the daisy, with only a few
petals to protect it as it rose humbly
towards the sun – and now the
plough has torn it from its bed
and laid it low.
*scanty mantle clad* = meagrely
covered; *snawie*= snowie;
*share uptears* = plough uproots;
*low thou lies* = you lie on the ground

Such is the fate of artless maid
Sweet flow'ret of the rural shade!
By lov's simplicity betray'd
And guileless trust,
Till she, like thee, all soil'd, is laid
Low i' the dust.

Such is the fate of the an innocent young maiden who has been betrayed by love and trust. She has nothing to look forward to until like the daisy, she shares its fate and death returns her to the dust.
*flow'ret* = little flower; *guilleless* = simple; *i'* = in

Such is the fate of simple Bard,
On life's rough ocean luckless starr'd
Unskilful he to note the card
Of prudent lore,
'Till billows rage, and gales blow hard,
And whelm him o'er.

The Bard had little luck throughout his lifetime, and has been neither sufficiently worldly nor prudent to avoid the storms of life which now threaten to overcome him.

Such fate to suffering worth is giv'n,
Who long with wants and woes has striv'n,
By human pride or cunning driv'n,
To mis'rys brink;
Till wrench'd of ev'ry stay but Heav'n
He, ruin'd, sink!

He is resigned to whatever fate has in store for him as his problems have driven him to the point of total despair. Everything in his life is bleak and there is little chance of salvation. Only ruination seems certain.
*wants and woes* = poverty and grief; *striv'n* = struggled; *ev'ry stay but Heav'n* = nothing left but death

Ev'n thou who mourn'st the Daisy's fate,
That fate is thine – no distant date;
Stern Ruin's plough-share drives elate,
Full on thy bloom
Till, crush'd beneath the furrow's weight
Shall be thy doom!

Finally, he compares the fate of the daisy to what is in store for himself as he believes that his own death is imminent. He sees no escape from the harshness of his life!
*elate* = proudly; *furrow's weight* = the earth turned over by the plough

# John Anderson, My Jo

This beautiful, simple old song tells the story of two people who have grown old together. However it did not start out this way and was in fact an old, bawdy ballad that the Bard breathed upon and revitalized.

John Anderson, my jo, John,
When we were first acquent;
Your locks were like the raven,
Your bonie brow was brent;
But now your brow is beld, John,
Your locks are like the snaw;
But blessings on your frosty pow
John Anderson, my jo.

The wife is reminding her husband that when they first met, his hair was as black as that of a raven and his brow was smooth and unlined. However, now he is almost bald and his few remaining locks are as white as the snow.
*jo* = sweetheart; *acquent* = acquainted; *locks* = hair; *brent* = smooth; *beld* = bald; *snaw*; snow; *frosty pow* = white head

John Anderson, my jo, John,
We clamb the hill thegither;
And mony a cantie day, John,
We've had wi' ane anither;
Now we maun totter down, John,
But hand in hand we'll go
And sleep thegither at the foot,
John Anderson, my jo

They have gone through life together and have had many happy days. Now as they approach the end of their lives, they still have each other.
*clamb* = climbed; *thegither* = together; *mony* = many; *cantie* = cheerful; *wi' ane anither* = with one another; *maun* = must; *totter* = stagger

# Her Flowing Locks

Here we have a snippet of a poem but we have no idea to whom it was to be dedicated or even when it was written. However, it is obvious that the Bard held this girl in high esteem.

Her flowing locks, the raven's wing,
Adown her neck and bosom hing;
How sweet unto that breast to cling,
And round that neck entwine her!

*the raven's wing* = as black as a raven
*Adown* = down; *hing* = hang

Her lips are roses wet wi' dew!
O, what a feast, her bonie mou!
Her cheeks a mair celestial hue,
A crimson still diviner

*wi'* = with
*bonie mou* = beautiful mouth
*mair* = more; *celestial* = heavenly
*still diviner* = even lovelier

# The Death and Dying Wishes of Poor Mailie

THE AUTHOR'S ONLY PET YOWE; AN UNCO MOURNFUL TALE

Burns had bought a ewe and her two lambs from a neighbouring farmer, really just to keeep as pets. The ewe was kept tethered in a field adjacent to his house.

Unfortunately, the ewe managed to entangle herself in her rope and fell into a ditch where she lay dying. The poem tells the story of the poor old ewe's dying wishes which she related to a passer-by who happened upon her as she lay there, but who was unable to be of any assistance.

This poem is one of the Bard's earliest works, if not his first to be written in the auld Scots tongue, and here the glossary is essential to the understanding of the poem.

As Mailie and her lambs thegither,
Was ae day nibblin' on the tether,
Upon her cloot she coost a hitch,
An' owre she warsl'd in the ditch;
There, groanin', dyin', she did lie,
When Hughoc he cam doytin by.

Mailie the ewe gets herself tangled in her tether and falls into the ditch where she is found by Hughoc, a none-too-bright farm labourer.

*thegither* = together; *ae* = one; *cloot* = hoof; *coost a hitch* = caught in a loop; *owre* = over; *warsl'd* = wrestled; *cam doytin by* = came doddering by

Wi' glowrin een, and lifted han's,
Poor Hughoc like a statue stan's;
He saw her days were near-hand ended,
But, waes my heart! He could na mend it!
He gaped wide, but naething spak,
At length poor Mailie silence brak.

Hughoc can only stand and stare, unable to move, and speechless until Mailie herself breaks the silence.

*Wi' glowrin een* = with staring eyes; *han's* = hands; *near-hand* = close by; *wae* = woe; *could na mend it* = could not help it; *naething spak* = said nothing; *brak* = broke

'O thou, whase lamentable face
Appears to mourn my woefu' case!
My dying words attentive hear,
And bear them to my Master dear.

She instructs him to listen to her
dying words and make certain
that he relates them to her master.
*whase* = whose; *lamentable* = sad;
*woefu' case* = deplorable state.

'Tell him, if e'er again he keep
As muckle gear as buy a sheep –
O, bid him never tie them mair,
Wi' wicked strings o' hemp or hair!
But ca' them out to park or hill,
An' let them wander at their will:
So may his flock increase an' grow
To scores o' lambs and packs o' woo' !

Should her master ever be able to
afford more sheep, then he is to
let them roam freely and nature
would increase the size of his
flock and produce more wool.
*muckle gear* = much wealth;
*mair* = anymore.

'Tell him he was a Master kin',
An' ay was guid to me an' mine;
An' now my dying charge I gie him,
My helpless lambs, I trust them wi' him.

Her dying wish is that her master
be responsible for the upbringing
of her lambs.
*kin'* = kind; *ay* = always.

'O, bid him save their harmless lives,
Frae dogs, an' tods, an' butcher's knives!
But gie them guid cow-milk their fill,
'Till they be fit to fend themsel';
An' tent them duly e'en an' morn,
Wi' taets o' hay an' ripps o' corn.

The master should ensure that the
lambs are not savaged by dogs or
foxes. He must not allow them to
be butchered, but must see that
they are fed carefully both
morning and night.
*tods* = foxes; *taets* = small
quantities; *ripps* = handfuls.

'An' may they never learn the gaets,
Of other vile, wanrestfu' pets –
To slink thro' slaps, an' reave an' steal
At stacks o' pease, or stocks o' kail!
So may they, like their great forbears,
For monie a year come thro' the sheers:
So wives will give them bits o' bread,
An' bairns greet for them when they're dead.

They must not become thieving
wastrels. With pride in their
ancestry they will supply wool for
years to come, and when they
die they will be sadly missed.
*gaets* = manners; *wanrestfu'* =
restless; *thro' slaps* = through gaps
in the hedges; *come thro' the sheers* =
be sheared; *greet* = cry

'My poor toop-lamb, my son an' heir,
O, bid him breed him up wi' care!
An' if he lives to be a beast,
To put some havins in his breast!

The eldest child must learn good
behaviour and grow up to be a
proud ram.
*toop* = tup; *put some havins* = put
some good manners

'An' warn him – what I winna name –
To stay content wi' yowes at hame;
An' no to rin an' wear his cloots,
Like ither menseless, graceless brutes.

He must stay with the flock, unlike
other ill–behaved oafs.
*no to rin* = not to run; *wear his
cloots* = wear out his hoofs

'An' niest, my yowie, silly thing,
Gude keep thee frae a tether string!
O, may thou ne'er forgather up,
Wi' onie blastit, moorland toop;
But ay keep mind to moop an' mell,
Wi' sheep o' credit like thysel'!

The silly baby ewe must be told to
watch out for tethers, and to
save herself for sheep of her own
class and not to get involved
with the wild rams which wander
the moorlands.
*niest* = next; *moop an' mell* = nibble
and mix.

'And now my bairns, wi' my last breath,
I lea'e my blessin wi' you baith;
An' when you think upo' your mither,
Mind to be kind to ane anither.

Mailie blesses her children and
reminds them to be kind to each
other.
*baith* = both

'Now, honest Hughoc, dinna fail,
To tell my master a' my tale;
An' bid him burn this curs'd tether,
An' for thy pains thou's got my blather.'

Hughoc must tell the master of her wishes and see to it that the tether is burned. His reward has been to hear her speak.

This said, poor Mailie turn'd her head,
An' clos'd her een amang the dead!

All this said, Mailie closes her eyes and dies.

# Poor Mailie's Elegy

Following the death of his pet sheep and his poem of her dying wishes, Burns now illustrates his own feelings about Mailie the ewe, and expresses his deep sorrow for her untimely departure from this earth.

Lament in rhyme, lament in prose,
Wi' saut tears trickling down your nose;
Our Bardie's fate is at a close,
Past a' remead!
The last sad cape-stane of his woes;
Poor Mailie's dead.

Burns' sorrow over the death of his pet sheep is obviously very deep.
*saut* = salt
*Past a' remead* = is incurable
*cape-stane* = cope-stone.

It's no the loss o' warl's gear,
That could sae bitter draw the tear,
Or mak our bardie, dowie, wear
The mourning weed:
He's lost a friend and neebor dear
In Mailie dead.

He does not regard her simply as a piece of property that he has lost, but believes her to have been a true friend and neighbour.
*warl's gear* = wordly wealth; *dowie* = sad; *mourning weed* = mourning clothes

Thro' a' the town she trotted by him,
Alang half-mile she could descry him;
Wi' kindly bleat, when she did spy him,
She ran wi' speed:
A friend mair faithfu' ne'er came nigh him,
Than Mailie dead.

He recalls how she would trot alongside him and how she could recognise him at a great distance.
*descry* = recognise
*ne'er came nigh* = never came close.

I wat she was a sheep o' sense,
An' could behave hersel' wi' mense;
I'll say't, she never brak a fence,
Thro' thievish greed,
Our Bardie, lanely keeps the spence
Sin' Mailie's dead.

She really was a sensible and graceful sheep who never attempted to break through into other fields to steal food.
*wat* = know; *mense* = good manners; *brak* = broke; *lanely* = lonely; *keeps the spence* = stays in the parlour.

Or, if he wanders up the howe,
Her living image in her yowe,
Comes bleating to him owre the knowe,
For bits o' bread;
An' down the briny pearls rowe
For Mailie dead.

The ewe lamb is so alike Mailie
that the Bard is reduced to tears
when she comes looking for bread,
just as her mother did.
*howe* = dell; *owre the knowe* =
over the hill; *briny pearls* = salty
tears; *rowe* = roll

She was nae get o' moorland tips,
Wi' tauted ket, an' hairy hips;
For her forbears were brought in ships,
'Frae yont the Tweed;
A bonnier fleesh ne'er cross'd the clips
Than Mailie's dead.

Mailie had good ancestry, unlike
the sheep that roamed the
moors. She came from foreign
parts and gave the finest wool.
*nae get o' moorlan' tips* = not
offspring of moorland rams; *wi'
tauted ket* = with matted fleece;
*a bonnier fleesh ne'er cross'd the clips* =
a better fleece was never sheared

Wae worth the man wha first did shape,
That vile wanchancie thing – a rape!
It maks guid fellows girn and gape,
Wi' chokin dread;
An' Robin's bonnet wave wi' crape
For Mailie dead.

He curses the first man to invent
the rope. Good men dread it, and
Burns is in mourning for Mailie
because of it.
*wae worth* = woe befall; *wha* =
who; *wanchancie* = unlucky;
*rape* = rope; *girn and gape* =
whimper and stare; *bonnet* = hat;
*wave wi' crape* = adorned with
black crepe

O, a' ye Bards on bonie Doon!
An' wha on Aire your chanters tune!
Come, join the melancholious croon
O' Robin's reed!
His heart will never get aboon!
His Mailie's dead!

Finally he calls on all poets and
pipers to join in a lament for
Mailie. He, Robert Burns, is
himself heart-broken – his Mailie
is dead.
*a' ye* = all you; *chanter* = bagpipes;
*melancholious croon* = lament;
*reed* = music pipe; *aboon* = above.

# Scotch Drink

*Gie him strong drink until he wink,*
*That's sinking in despair;*
*An' liquor guid to fire his bluid,*
*That's prest wi' grief and care;*
*There let bowse, and deep carouse,*
*Wi' bumpers flowing o'er,*
*Till he forgets his loves or debts,*
*An' minds his griefs no more.*

SOLOMON'S PROVERBS, CH XXXI, VERSES 6&7

Here we have fairly lengthy poem dedicated to the virtues of Scotch whisky, and at the same time taking the opportunity to slam the imposition of tax upon such a popular drink. (Nothing really changes in life.)

It would appear that illegal stills were not uncommon in those distant days, and the excisemen also come under attack for their constant pursuit of illicit distillers.

Let other poets raise a fracas,
'Bout vines and wines, and drucken Bacchus,
An' crabbit names an' stories wrack us,
An' grate our lug;
I sing the juice Scotch bear can make us,
In glass or jug.

Burns has no interest in the praise of wines, or in listening to others tell tales of Bacchus. For him, the only true drink comes from the barley of Scotland – whisky.
*drucken* = drunken; *crabbit* = ill-natured; *wrack* = punish; *grate our lug* = irritate our ear; *bear* = barley

Thou, my Muse! Guid auld Scotch drink!
Whether thro' wimplin worms thou jink,
Or richly brown, ream owre the brink,
In glorious faem.
Inspire me, till I lisp an' wink,
To sing thy name!

As the whisky winds its way through the coils of the distilling apparatus, he is inspired by the rich, brown liquid foaming in the still.
*wimplin* = waving; *jink* = dodge; *ream* = froth; *faem* = foam

63

Let husky wheat the haughs adorn,
An' aits set up their awnie horn,
An' pease and beans at e'en or morn,
Perfume the plain:
Leeze me on thee, John Barleycorn,
Thou king o' grain!

The Bard has no objection to the
sight of fields of wheat, oats,
peas and beans, but nevertheless
his blessings are given to barley,
the king of grain.
*haughs* = meadows; *aits* = oats;
*awnie* = bearded; *pease* = peas
*leeze on thee* = blessings on you;
*John Barleycorn* = whisky.

On thee aft Scotland chows her cood,
In souple scones, the wale o' food!
Or tumbling in the boiling flood
Wi' kail an' beef;
But when thou pours thy strong heart's blood,
There thou shines chief.

Although Scotland depends on
barley for the making of favourite
scones, or to thicken up the soup,
it is only when in liquid form
that its true value is revealed.
*aft* = often; *chows her cood* = eats
her food; *souple scones* = soft
barley cakes; *wale* = choice,
*kail* = cabbage

Food fills the wame an' keeps us livin';
Tho' life's a gift no' worth receivin',
When heavy dragg'd wi' pine an' grievin';
But oil'd by thee,
The wheels o' life gae down-hill, scrievin',
Wi' rattlin' glee.

We are all aware that food fills our
bellies and keeps us alive, but
life can seem to be nothing more
than burdensome, weary toil,
and whisky can help make that life
much more cheerful.
*wame* = belly; *leivin'* = living, *heavy
dragg'd* = worn out, *wi' pine an'
grievin;* = with suffering and grieving;
*scrievin'* = gliding easily; *rattlin'* = lively

Thou clears the head o' doited Lear,
Thou cheers the heart o' drooping Care,
Thou strings the nerves o' Labour sair,
At's weary toil;
Thou ev'n brightens dark Despair
Wi' gloomy smile.

Whisky can clear muddled heads
as well as help dispel care and
pain. Even the deepest despair can
be lightened with a glass of
whisky.
*doited lear* = stupid lore

Aft, clad in massy siller weed,
Wi' gentles thou erects thy head;
Yet humbly kind in times o' need,
The poor man's wine;
His wee drap parritch, or his bread,
Thou kitchens fine.

The gentry may serve their whisky in fancy silver cups, but it can always be relied on to be the poor man's wine and to supplement his meagre meal.
*clad in massy siller weed* = dressed in heavy silver; *gentles* = gentry; *wee drap parritch* = small drop of porridge; *kitchens* = makes palatable

Thou art the life o' public haunts;
But thee, what were our fairs and rants?
Ev'n godly meetings o' the saunts,
By thee inspir'd,
When gaping, they besiege the tents,
Are doubly fir'd.

How dull life would be without whisky. Festivals and Fairs are much livelier when it is present, and the tents where it is sold are always thronged with thirsty people.
*public haunts* = taverns; *what were our fairs and rants* = that was our pleasure and joy; *saunts* = saints; *fir'd* = affected

That merry night we get the corn in,
O sweetly then, thou reams the horn in!
Or reekin' on a New Year mornin'
In cog or bicker,
An' just a wee drap sp'ritual burn in,
An' gusty sucker!

Harvest time is always cause for celebration, but on New Year's morning, whisky is especially enjoyed steaming hot, with a drop of water from the burn and a touch of sugar.
*reams the horn in* = froths in the cup; *reekin'* = smoking; *cog or bicker* = wooden dishes; *gusty sucker* = sugar

When Vulcan gies his bellows breath,
An' ploughmen gather wi' their graith.
O rare! To see thee fizz an' freath
I' th' lugget caup!
Then Burnewin come on like death,
At ev'ry chaup.

When ploughmen gather at he smithy, the whisky froths in the cup, and the blacksmith hammers more heartily after a drop.
*When Vulcan gies his bellows breath* = in the heat of the smithy; *graith* = harness; *fizz an' freath* = hiss and froth; *lugget caup* = a two-handled cup; *Burnewin* = blacksmith; *chaup* = blow

Nae mercy then for airn or steel;
The brawnie, bainie, ploughman chiel,
Brings hard owrehip, wi' sturdy wheel,
The strong forehammer,
'Till block an' studdie ring an' reel
Wi' dinsome clamour.

With no mercy for the iron or steel on which he is working, the blacksmith's muscular forearm causes his hammer to make the anvil ring out aloud.
*airn* = iron; *bainie* = muscular; *chiel* = young man; *owrehip* = a method of hammering; *block an' studdie* = anvil and smithy; *dinsome* = noisy

When skirlin' weanies see the light,
Thou maks the gossips clatter bright,
How fumblin' cuifs their dearies slight,
Wae worth the name!
Nae howdie gets a social night,
Or plack frae them.

While celebrating a new baby with a drop of whisky, the women gossip about their husbands and forget to reward the midwife.
*skirlin' weanies* = shrieking babies; *clatter bright* = talking noisily; *fumblin' cuifs* = awkward fools, *dearies slight* = insult their loved ones; *wae worth* = woe befall, *howdie* = midwife; *plack* = small coin

When neebors anger at a plea,
An' just as wud as wud can be,
How easy can the barley-brie
Cement the quarrel!
It's aye the cheapest lawyer's fee,
To taste the barrel,

Here the Bard speaks words of
wisdom as he points out that it is
far cheaper to have a drink with a
neighbour to resolve a quarrel,
than to pay the fees of a lawyer.
*neebors* = neighbours; *wud* = mad;
*barley-brie* = whisky; *aye* = always

Alake! That e'er my Muse has reason,
To wyte her countrymen wi' treason!
But monie daily weet their weason
Wi' liquors nice.
An' hardly, in a winter season,
E'er spier her price.

Sad to say, but we have reason to
accuse some of our countrymen
of treason because they consume
drinks other than whisky – and
they do not even ask the price.
*Alake* = alas; *wyte* = blame; *weet
their weason* = wet their throat;
*spier* = ask

Wae worth that brandy, burnin' trash!
Fell source o' monie a pain an' brash!
Twins monie a poor doylt, drucken hash
O' half his days;
An' sends, beside, auld Scotland's cash
To her warst faes.

Brandy is trash which causes
painful hangovers and is the reason
for so many lost working-days.
What's more, the revenue from
brandy goes to support the
country's enemies.
*fell* = biting; *brash* = sickness;
*twins* = deprives; *doylt drucken
hash* = stupid, drunken fellow;
*warst faes* = worst foes

Ye Scots, wha wish auld Scotland well!
Ye chief, to you my tale I tell,
Poor, plackless devils like mysel'!
It sets you ill,
Wi' bitter dearthfu' wines to mell,
Or foreign gill.

If you wish Scotland well, then do
not bother with fancy, foreign
wines – they will do you no good
at all.
*chief* = mainly; *plackless* = penniless;
*dearthfu'* = expensive; *mell* = to
meddle; *gill* = a measure of whisky

May gravels round his blather wrench,
An' gouts torment him, inch by inch,
Wha twists his gruntle wi' a grunch
O' sour disdain,
Out owre a glass o' whisky-punch
Wi' honest men!

May anyone who dares sneer at a man who enjoys a glass of whisky with his friends have a bladder that feels like gravel, and suffer from gout.
*may gravels round his blather wrench* = may kidney-stones give him pains in his bladder; *twists his gruntle wi' a grunch* = screws his face up in a frown

O Whisky! soul o' plays an' pranks!
Accept a Bardie's gratefu' thanks!
When wanting thee, what tuneless cranks
Are my poor verses!
Thou comes – they rattle i' their ranks,
At ither's arses!

Burns acknowledges that his verses are often tuneless noises until he has had a glass of whisky, then the words come pouring out.
*plays and pranks* = games and jokes; *cranks* = creakings; *ither's arses* = other's backsides

Thee Ferintosh! O sadly lost!
Scotland lament frae coast to coast!
Now colic grips, an' barkin' hoast
May kill us a',
For loyal Forbes' chartered boast
Is ta'en awa'!

In reparation for damage done during the Jacobite Rebellion, Ferintosh Distillery (owned by the Forbes family) had been freed from paying excise duty. This privilege was withdrawn in 1785, and the price of whisky escalated rapidly, depriving men of their favourite tipple.
*colic grips* = illness takes hold; *barkin' hoast* = barking cough; *ta'en awa'* = taken away

Thae curst  horse-leeches o' the Excise,
Wha mak the whisky stells their prize!
Haud up thy han', Deil, ance, twice, thrice!
There seize the blinkers!
An' bake them up in brunstane pies
For poor damn'd drinkers.

Closing illicit stills was one of the
main activities of the despised
exciseman, and the Devil is called
upon to deal with them harshly.
*horse-leeches* = blood-suckers;
*stells* = stills; *haud up thy han'* =
hold up your hand; *blinkers* = a form
of contempt; *brunstane* = brimstone

Fortune! If thou'll but gie me still
Hale breeks, a scone, an' whisky gill,
An' rowth o' rhyme to rave at will,
Tak a' the rest,
An' deal't about as thy blind skill
Directs the best.

All the Bard wants from life are
whole trousers, some food to eat
along with his whisky, and some
rhyme to produce at will. With
these he can accept whatever life
has in store for him.
*Hale breeks* = whole trousers;
*rowth o'* = abundance of; *rave* = utter

# The Gowden Locks of Anna

At first glance it would appear that this song is yet another of the Bard's works intended to flatter one of his lady loves. However, written around 1790, it actually relates to a very significant episode in his life.

Although married to Jean Armour at the time, Burns was having an affair with a lass by the name of Anne Park, the niece of the landlady of the Globe Inn in Dumfries. This affair ended tragically as Anne died giving birth to a daughter, leaving Burns to present his wife with his illegimate child a mere nine days before she herself gave birth to a son. Jean Armour must have been a truly remarkable person, as she accepted young Elizabeth into her family and raised her as her own child.

The words need no explanation. They speak clearly of Burns' feelings at the time.

Yestreen I had a pint o' wine,
A place where body saw na;
Yestreen lay on this breast o' mine
The gowden locks of Anna.
The hungry Jew in wilderness
Rejoicing o'er his manna,
Was naething to my hiney bliss
Upon the lips of Anna.

*Yestreen* = yesterday;
*body saw na* = nobody saw
anything; *gowden* = golden;
*manna* = food of the Israelites in
the wilderness; *naething* = nothing;
*hiney* = honey

Ye Monarchs take the East and West,
Frae Indus to Savannah!
Gie me within my straining grasp
The melting form of Anna.
There I'll despise Imperial charms,
An Empress or Sultana,
While dying raptures in her arms
I give and take with Anna!!!

Awa thou flaunting God of Day!
Awa, thou pale Diana!                              *Diana* = the moon goddess
Ilk Star gae hide thy twinkling ray              *Ilk* = each
When I'm to meet my Anna!
Come in thy raven plumage, Night;
Sun, moon and stars withdrawn a';
And bring an angel pen to write
My transports wi' my Anna.                       *transports* = ecstasies


*Postscript*


The kirk and state may join and tell,            *kirk* = church
To do sic things I manna;                         *sic* = such; *manna* = must not
The kirk and state can go to hell,
And I shall gae to Anna.
She is the sunshine o' my e'e,
To live but her I canna;                          *To live but her I canna* = I cannot live
Had I on earth but wishes three,                 without her
The first should be my Anna.

# On Glenriddell's Fox Breaking His Chain

Captain Robert Riddell was a very good friend of Robert Burns, but to the disgust of the poet, he kept a fox chained to a kennel. Burns was totally against the keeping of any wild animal in captivity, and when the fox managed to break its chain and escape, he was inspired to write the following lines in which the thoughts of freedom are the main theme.

Thou, Liberty, thou art my theme;
Not such as idle poets dream,
Who trick thee up a heathen goddess
That fantastic cap and rod has!
Such stale conceits are poor and silly:
I paint thee out a Highland filly,
A sturdy, stubborn, handsome dapple,
As sleek's a mouse, as round's an apple,
That when thou pleasest can do wonders,
But when thy luckless rider blunders,
Or if thy fancy should demur there,
Wilt break thy neck ere thou go further.

Burns refuses to consider the idea of Liberty being represented by some strangely clad goddess. No. He saw her as a beautiful Highland pony that would never allow captivity to break her spirit.
*trick thee up* = dress you up; *stale conceits* = overused pretences; *demur* = hesitate

These things premis'd, I sing a Fox –
Was caught among his native rocks,
And to a dirty kennel chained –
How he his liberty regained.

He tells of the fox being caught, but also of it eventually regaining its freedom.
*premis'd* = assumed

Glenriddell! A Whig without a stain,
A Whig in principle and grain,
Coulds't thou enslave a free-born creature,
A native denizen of Nature?
How coulds't thou with heart so good
(A better was ne'er sluiced with blood)
Nail a poor devil to a tree,
That ne'er did harm to thine or thee?

He asks his friend, Glenriddell, a man of truth and principle, how such a kind-hearted person could ever hold an animal in captivity, especially as the fox has done no harm to him or his family.
*grain* = moral fibre; *denizen* = inhabitant

The staunchest Whig Glenriddell was,
Quite frantic in his country's cause,
And oft was Reynard's prison passing,
And with his brother-Whigs canvassing,
The rights of men, the power of women,
With all the dignity of Freemen.

Glenriddell was a staunch Whig, regularly discussing the rights of men and women with his political allies as they passed by the fox's kennel. But they were free men while the fox was a prisoner.

*Reynard* = fox; *canvassing* = discussing

Sir Reynard daily heard debates
Of princes, kings', and nation's fates,
With many rueful, bloody stories
Of tyrants, Jacobites and Tories;
From liberty how angels fell,
That are now galley-slaves in Hell;

Each day during his captivity, the fox heard debates on mans' inhumanity to man. An incredible range of topics fell upon his ever attentive ears, ranging from mythology to historical facts, from the ravagings of the Roman Empire to the imposition of income tax by William Pitt.

How Nimrod first the trade began
Of binding Slavery's chains on man;
How fell Semiramis – God damn her!
Did first with sacriligious hammer
(all ills till then were trivial matters).
For Man dethron'd forge hen-peck fetters;
How Xerces, that abandoned Tory,
Thought cutting throats was reaping glory,
Until the stubborn Whigs of Sparta
Taught him great Nature's Magna Charta:
How mighty Rome her fiat hurl'd
Resistless o'er a bowing world.
And kinder than they did desire,
Polish'd mankind with sword and fire:
With much too tedious to relate
Of ancient and of modern date,
But ending still, how Billy Pitt
(Unlucky boy!) with wicked wit
Has gagg'd old Britain, drain'd her coffer,
As butchers bind and bleed a heifer.

Thus wily Reynard, by degrees,
In kennel listening at his ease,
Suck'd in a mighty stock of knowledge,
As much as some folks at a college;
Knew Britain's rights and constitution,
Her aggrandizement, diminution;
How Fortune wrought us good from evil;
Let no man then, despise the Devil,
As who should say 'I ne'er can need him.'
Since we to scoundrels owe our freedom.

By the time the fox made his escape, he had absorbed as much information as a college graduate, but he also learned that tyrants and other evil people are the reason that the British set such high store on freedom.

*suck'd in* = absorbed
*aggrandizement* = making great
*diminution* = lessening
*wrought* = fashioned

# Lines Written on a Bank Note

The following lines were actually written upon a one-guinea note in 1786. At the time, Burns was giving a good deal of thought to the idea of emigrating to Jamaica believing that this might be a means of escaping from his ever-present problems.

Many of us will have little difficulty in relating to the heart-felt words of this poem.

Wae worth thy power, thou cursed leaf!     *Wae worth* = woe befall
Fell source of a' my woe and grief,     *Fell source* = cause
For lack of thee I've lost my lass,
For lack o' thee I scrimp my glass!     *scrimp my glass* = limit my drinking
I see the children of affliction
Unaided, through your curs'd restriction.
I've seen the oppressor's cruel smile
Amid his hapless victim's spoil;
And for thy potence vainly wish'd     *potence* = power
To crush the villain in the dust.
For lack o' thee I leave this much-lov'd shore,
Never, perhaps, to greet old Scotland more.

# Bonie Wee Thing

As we read the many beautiful poems and songs which Burns composed over the years, we must marvel at his ability to use his verse as a means of flattering whichever young woman had caught his eye. This particular song was dedicated to a lass by the name of Deborah Duff Davies, who was also the recipient of several letters from the Bard. Although I have no idea whether or not Burns was successful in his pursuit of Miss Davies, I do know that this song has become one of his best-loved works, and expect that it will remain so for many years to come.

Bonie wee thing, Cannie wee thing,　　　　*Bonie* = beautiful; *Cannie* = gentle
Lovely wee thing, wert thou mine,
I wad wear thee in my bosom　　　　*wad* = would
Lest my jewel I should tine.　　　　*tine* = lose


Wistfully I look and languish,
In that bonie face o' thine;
And my heart it stounds wi' anguish,　　　　*stounds* = pains
Lest my wee thing na be mine.　　　　*na* = not


Wit, and grace, and love, and beauty,
In ae constellation shine;
To adore thee is my duty,
Goddess o' this soul o' mine.

# The Henpecked Husband

This is a very straightforward, no-holds-barred poem by the Bard, leaving us in no doubt as to his thoughts upon nagging wives.


Curs'd be the man, the poorest wretch in life,
The crouching vassal to the tyrant wife!    *vassal* = slave
Who has no will but by her high permission;
Who has no sixpence but in her possession;
Who must to her his dear friend's secrets tell;
Who dreads a curtain lecture worse than hell.    *curtain lecture* = a lecture given in
Were such the wife had fallen to my part,    bed by a wife to her husband
I'd break her spirit, or I'd break her heart.
I'd charm her with the magic of a switch,    *switch* = cane
I'd kiss her maids, and kick the perverse bitch.

# I'll Go and be a Sodger

Robert Burns must have experienced an incredible variety of lifestyles. Here he is, twenty-three years old, with ruin staring him in the face. His business partner in a flax-dressing shop had defrauded him, and on top of that, while indulging in the New Year festivities, his shop burned down. Little wonder that he contemplated a career in the army.

O why the deuce should I repine,
And be an ill-foreboder?
I'm twenty-three and five feet nine,
I'll go and be a sodger!

*deuce* = devil; *repine* = feel discontent; *ill-foreboder* = a forecaster of misfortune; *sodger* = soldier

I gat some gear wi' meikle care,
I held it weel thegither;
But now it's gane – and something mair;
I'll go and be a sodger!

*gear* = wealth; *meikle* = much; *weel thegither* = well together; *gane* = gone; *mair* = more.

# Address to the Unco Guid
## or the Rigidly Righteous

*My son, these maxims make a rule*
*An' bump them a' thegither;*
*The Rigid Righteous is a fool,*
*The Rigid Wise anither;*
*The cleanest corn that e'er was dig*
*May have some piles o' caff in;*
*So ne'er a fellow creature slight*
*For random fits o' daffin,*

SOLOMON, ECCLESIASTES, CH VII, VERSE 16

Robert Burns was never one to tolerate the 'Holier Than Thou' attitude held by so many during his lifetime (and still as common today). It was his belief that all men, even those considered to be blackguards, had some good to offer society, and that we should never consider ourselves to so morally superior to anyone that we may be blinded by our own self-importance, for some day, we may be the ones being looked down upon.

O ye, wha are sae guid yoursel'
Sae pious and sae holy,
Ye've naught to do but mark and tell
Your neebour's fauts and folly!
Whase life is like a weel-gaun mill,
Supplied wi store o' water;
The heapet happer's ebbing still,
An' still the clap plays clatter!

Self-righteous people believe their orderly lives permit them to criticise others who they believe to have inferior standards of behaviour. *wha are sae guid* = who are so good; *naught* = nothing; *neebour* = neighbour; *fauts and folly* = faults and foolishness; *whase* = whose; *weel-gaun* = good-going; *heapet happer* = heaped hopper; *ebbing* = sinking; *plays clatter* = acts noisily

Hear me, ye venerable core,
As counsel for poor mortals
That frequent pass douce Wisdom's door
For glaikit Folly's portals;
I for their thoughtless, careless, sakes,
Would here propone defences –
Their donsie tricks, their black mistakes,
Their failings and mischances.

Burns offers a defence for those
who might have been foolish in
their lives, whose sexual adventures
may have caused them some regret,
and who are generally regarded as
failure by society.
*venerable core* = revered company;
*douce* = grave; *glaikit* = foolish;
*propone* = propose; *donsie tricks* =
sick pranks; *mischances* = ill-luck

You see your state wi' theirs compared,
And shudder at the niffer;
But cast a moment's fair regard,
What makes the mighty differ?
Discount what scant occasion gave;
The purity ye pride in;
And (what's aft mair than a' the lave)
Your better art o' hidin'.

The self-righteous may shudder at
being compared with such people,
but often the only difference is
that they have been more
successful in concealing their
transgressions, or perhaps they may
never have been put to the test.
*niffer* = comparison
*scant occasion* = slight opportunity
*aft mair* = often more
*a' the lave* = all the rest

Think, when your castigated pulse
Gies now and then a wallop,
What ragings must his veins convulse,
That still eternal gallop!
Wi' wind and tide fair i' your tail,
Right on ye scud your sea-way,
But in the teeth o' baith to sail,
It maks an unco lee-way.

He asks them to remember how
they feel when their pulses race,
and to consider how it might be for
someone with little control over
their feelings. He suggests that
while they may be fine when all is
going their way, they may react
differently in the face of adversity.
*castigated* = chastised; *scud* = drive
before the wind; *baith* = both;
*an unco lee-way* = uncommonly
hard-going.

See Social Life and Glee sit down,
All joyous and unthinking,
Till, quite transmugrify'd they're grown
Debauchery and Drinking;
O, would they stay to calculate
Th' eternal consequences,
Or, your more dreaded hell to state –
Damnation of expenses!

While ordinary people regard socialising as an occasion for enjoyment, the self-righteous tend to see such happenings as deeply sinful, and therefore a direct path to hell.

*transmugrify'd* = transformed

Ye high, exalted, virtuous dames,
Tied up in godly laces,
Before ye gie poor Frailty names,
Suppose a change o' cases;
A dear lov'd lad, convenience snug.
A treach'rous inclination –
But let me whisper i' your lug,
Ye're aiblins nae temptation.

Burns then questions how the good ladies, all tied up in their corsets would react if offered the opportunity for pleasure with someone they admired deeply, but then cuttingly doubts if they would be capable of attracting any man.

*snug* = sheltered; *aiblins* = perhaps

Then gently scan your brother man,
Still gentler sister woman;
Tho' they may gang a kennin wrang,
To step aside is human:
One point must still be greatly dark,
The moving, why they do it;
And just as lamely can ye mark,
How far perhaps they rue it.

He asks that consideration and forgiveness be given to one's fellow man and woman who may have erred in life. Without knowing what prompted them to have sinned in the first place, there is no knowing the sorrow and regret that a person may now be suffering.

*a kennin* = a little bit

*wrang* = wrong

Who made the heart, 'tis He alone
Decidedly can try us;
He knows each cord, its various tone,
Each spring, its various bias;
Then at the balance, let's be mute,
We never can adjust it;
What's done we partly may compute,
But know not what's resisted.

Only God has the ability to judge
us. Only He knows the full story.
Although we may have witnessed
some transgressions, we have no
way of knowing how many others
have been resisted.

# The Tree of Liberty

Here we have another poem by the Burns on one of his favourite topics – liberty. This poem appears to have been inspired by the French Revolution, but the Bard's sympathies obviously lie toward the Jacobite cause.

Heard ye o' the Tree o' France,
I watna what's the name o't,
Around it a' the patriots dance,
Weel Europe kens the fame o't.
It stands where ance the Bastile stood,
A prison built by kings, man,
When superstition's hellish brood
Kept France in leading strings, man.

By use of the term, the 'Tree o' France', the Bard symbolises liberty and freedom. The storming of the infamous Bastille in Paris, and its subsequent use as a prison for the aristocracy before its destruction, marked the beginning of freedom for the oppressed peasants of France.
*watna* = don't know; *kens* = knows; *ance* = once; *leading strings* = reins

Upo' this tree there grows sic fruit,
Its virtues I can tell, man;
It raises man aboon the brute,
It maks him ken himsel, man,
Gif ance the peasant taste a bit,
He's greater than a lord, man,
An' wi' the beggar shares a mite
O' a' he can afford, man.

Freedom is a virtue that raises man above the beast. A peasant who tastes freedom will be a better man than a lord, for he has known poverty and oppression and will be more inclined to help those who have nothing.
*upo'* = upon; *sic* = such; *aboon* = above; *Gif* = if; *ance* = once

This fruit is worth a' Afric's wealth,
To comfort us 'twas sent, man;
To gie the sweetest blush o' health,
An' mak us a' content, man;
It clears the een, it cheers the heart,
Maks high and low gude friends, man;
And he wha acts the traitor's part
It to perdition sends, man.

Freedom is worth all the wealth to be found in Africa. A free man has clearness of vision, and with happiness in his heart can befriend people in all levels of society. Only ruination will come to those who oppose freedom.
*gie* = give; *een* = eyes; *gude* = good; *perdition* = hell

My blessings aye attend the chiel
Wha pitied Gallia's slaves, man
And staw a branch, spite o' the deil,
Frae yont the western waves, man.
Fair Virtue water'd it wi' care,
And now she sees wi' pride, man
How weel it buds and blossoms there,
Its branches spreading wide, man.

Burns blesses the person responsible for the start of the French Revolution, and casts his eye to America where the seeds of discontent concerning the slave trade are growing rapidly.

*aye* = always; *chiel* = young man; *Gallia* = France; *staw* = stole; *frae yont* = from beyond; *weel* = well

Buit vicious folk aye hate to see
The works o' Virtue thrive, man;
The courtly vermin's banned the tree,
And grat to see it thrive, man;
King Loui' thought to cut it down,
When it was unco sma', man;
For this the watchman cracked his crown,
Cut off his head and a', man.

Not everyone is enthusiastic about the rights of man. The French ruling classes did their utmost to suppress the peasants when revolt threatened, but the ultimate result was that King Louis XVI was beheaded by the very people that he had persecuted.

*grat* = wept; *unco sma'* = very small

A wicked crew syne on a time,
Did tak a solemn aith, man,
It ne'er should flourish to its prime,
I wat they pledged their faith, man.
Awa' they gaed wi' mock parade,
Like beagles hunting game, man,
But soon grew weary o' the trade
And wished they'd been at hame, man

Supporters of the aristocracy attempted in desperation to fight back and to reinstate the slave-like conditions to which the peasants had been subjected, but they soon realised that the battle was lost.

*syne* = once; *aith* = oath; *wat* = know; *gaed* = went; *hame* = home

For Freedom, standing by the tree,
Her sons did loudly ca', man;
She sang a song o' liberty,
Which pleased them ane and a', man.
By her inspired, the new-born race
Soon drew the avenging steel, man;
The hirelings ran – her foes gied chase,
And banged the despot weel, man

Inspired by the stirring words of La Marseillaise, the peasant uprising saw the end of the despotic ruling classes throughout the whole of France.
*ca'* = call; *ane and a'* = one and all; *gied* = gave; *banged the despot weel* = struck a heavy blow against the tyrant

Let Britain boast her hardy oak,
Her poplar and her pine, man,
Auld Britain ance could crack her joke,
And o'er her neighbours shine, man,
But seek the forest round and round,
And soon 'twill be agreed, man,
That sic a tree can not be found,
'Twixt London and the Tweed, man.

The Bard points out that although many trees grow throughout Britain, there is no Tree of Liberty. Freedom no longer exists and the people are again no more than serfs.
*auld* = old; *ance* = once; *crack* = tell

Without this tree, alake this life
Is but a vale o' woe, man;
A scene o' sorrow mixed wi' strife,
Nae real joys we know, man.
We labour soon, we labour late,
To feed the titled knave, man;
And a' the comfort we're to get
Is that ayont the grave, man.

Life without freedom is a joyless existence, where the working man knows nothing but endless toil trying to meet the demands of his titled master. Only death will relieve him of his burden.
*alake* = alas; *ayont* = beyond

Wi' plenty o' sic trees I trow,
The warld would live in peace, man;
The sword would help to mak a plough,
The din o' war wad cease, man;
Like brethren in a common cause,
We'd on each other smile, man;
And equal rights and equal laws
Wad gladden every isle, man.

If all men were free with equal rights, then war would be a thing of the past. Weapons could be turned into ploughs and mankind could go forward together.
*trow* = believe; *warld* = world; *din* = noise

Wae worth the loon wha wadna eat
Sic halesome dainty cheer, man;
I'd gie my shoon frae off my feet,
To taste sic fruit, I swear, man.
Syne let us pray, auld England may
Sure plant this far-famed tree, man;
And blythe we'll sing, and hail the day
That gave us liberty, man.

Burns would give the shoes of his
feet to see this happening. He
prays for the day when Scotland
will be free from the English
yoke and Scotsmen can sing the
song of liberty.

*wae worth the loon* = woe befall
the rascal; *wha wadna* = who
would not; *hoon* = shoes;
*frae aff* = from off; *blythe* = cheerfully

# Jessie

Once again we have yet another example of the Bard's amazing ability to flatter young women in verse. On this occasion the subject was Jessie Staig, the daughter of the provost of Dumfries. She died in 1801 at the age of twenty-six. Jessie must have been seventeen or eighteen when the song was written, and Burns recognised that, although she was truly beautiful, she was also an extremely modest young lady.

True-hearted was he, the sad swain o' the Yarrow,     *swain* = lover
And fair are the maids on the banks o' the Ayr,
But by the sweet side o' the Nith's winding river,
Are lovers as faithful, and maidens as fair;
To equal young Jessie seek Scotland all over;
To equal young Jessie you seek it in vain;
Grace beauty and elegance fetter her lover,     *fetter* = restrain
And maidenly modesty fixes the chain.


O, fresh is the rose in the gay, dewy morning,
And sweet is the lily at evening close;
But in the fair presence o' lovely young Jessie,
Unseen is the lily, unheeded the rose.
Love sits in her smile, a wizard ensnaring;
Enthron'd in her een he delivers his law;     *een* = eyes
And still to her charms she alone is a stranger!
Her modest demeanour's the jewel of a'.     *a'* = all

# Auld Lang Syne

This is certainly the most famous song to come from the pen of Robert Burns, the inspiration coming from an old Scots ballad. Sung at gatherings throughout the world, particularly at the beginning of each New Year, Auld Lang Syne has become an international anthem, as people of all creeds and colours join hands in celebration. However, very few people actually know the words they are endeavouring to sing, and even fewer understand the meaning and relevance of these words. Indeed in too many instances it is a signal for the start of drunken revelry, rather than a gentle reminder to spend a few moments thinking of friends of long ago. I can only hope that when you have read the words and understand what Burns was really saying, that you will give the song the respect which it truly deserves.

*Chorus*
*For auld lang syne, my dear,*
*For auld lang syne,*
*We'll tak' a cup o' kindness yet,*
*For auld lang syne.*

| | |
|---|---|
| Should auld acquaintance be forgot, | The message is that we should |
| And never brought to min'? | never forget old friends. |
| Should auld acquaintance be forgot, | *auld* = old; *min'* = mind; |
| And auld lang syne. | *lang syne* = of long ago |

| | |
|---|---|
| And surely ye'll be your pint-stowp! | Let us raise our glasses in toast to |
| And surely I'll be mine! | these memories. |
| And we'll tak a cup o' kindness yet, | *stowp* = drinking vessel; *tak* = take |
| For auld lang syne. | |

| | |
|---|---|
| We twa hae run about the braes, | We played together, but grew up |
| And pu'd the gowans fine; | and went our own ways. |
| But we've wandered mony a weary fit | *twa* = two; *hae* = have; *braes* = hills; |
| Sin' auld lang syne. | *pu'd the gowans* = pulled he daisies; |
| | *mony a weary foot* = travelled great |
| | distances |

We twa hae paidl't i' the burn,
Frae mornin' sun till dine;
But seas between us braid hae roar'd
Sin' auld lang syne.

As children, we paddled in the
stream, but since then we have
been separated by the width of the
oceans.
*paidl't i' the burn* = paddled in
the burn; *frae mornin' sun till dine* =
all day; *braid* = broad

And there's a hand, my trusty fiere!
And gie's a hand o' thine!
And we'll tak a right guid-willie waught,
For auld lang syne.

Shake my hand my trusted friend
and let us share a goodwill drink to
the memory of these happy days.
*fiere* = friend; *a right guid-willie
waught* = a goodwill drink

# The Cotter's Saturday Night

INSCRIBED TO R. AIKEN, ESQ.

*Let not ambition mock their useful toil,*
*Their homely joys, and destiny obscure;*
*Nor grandeur hear; with a disdainful smile,*
*The short and simple annals of the poor.*

THOMAS GRAY

Cotters, or cottagers were the labouring classes of the farming community, the people who dug the ditches and cleared the stones from the fields. People to whom life was an ongoing struggle against poverty and starvation, and yet were the people for whom Burns had a burning respect and admiration. Proud, proud people who were both God -fearing and law-abiding citizens, and whose aspirations were seldom greater than to be allowed to feed and house their families. Once again the Bard presents himself as a true champion of the working-classes, displaying his contempt for the paraphernalia of church and state. Burns wrote this wonderful poem when he was twenty-six years old, and dedicated it to Robert Aiken, one of the targets of Holy Willie's venomous tirades, and to whom the poem is addressed in the opening lines. It is interesting to note that at his relatively young age he uses a quote from Alexander Pope, who died fifteen years before Burns was born; 'An honest man's the noblest work of God'. So much for the stories of the illiterate ploughman.

My lov'd, my honour'd, much respected friend!
No mercenary bard his homage pays;
With honest pride I scorn each selfish end,
My dearest meed, a friend's esteem and praise;
To you I sing in simple Scottish lays,
The lowly train in life's sequester'd scene;
The native feelings strong, the guileless ways;
What Aiken in a cottage would have been:
Ah! tho' his worth unknown,
        far happier there, I ween.

The poem starts with Burns paying his respects to Robert Aiken, explaining to him that had he been born a cottager, then this is how life would have been, and telling him that he may have been a happier man for it.

*meed* = reward; *lay* = song;
*ween* = expect

November chill blaws loud wi' angry sough;
The short'ning winter-day is near a close;
The miry beasts retreating frae the pleugh;
The black'ning trains o' craws to their repose;
The toil-worn Cotter frae his labour goes –
This night his weekly moil is at an end,
Collects his spades, his mattocks, and his hoes,
Hoping the morn in ease and rest to spend,
And weary o'er the moor, his course does
    hameward bend.

The scene changes to the cotter wearily returning homewards on a Saturday evening, hoping to spend the following morning resting his tired body. The returning horses, covered in mud from the ploughing, and the masses of crows flying to their nests paints a very vivid picture.
*blaws* = blows; *sough* = sigh; *miry* = muddy; *frae the pleugh* = from the plough; *trains o' craws* = spoil of crows; *moil* = labour *mattock* = pickaxe; *hameward* = homeward

At length his lonely cot appears in view,
Beneath the shelter of an aged tree;
Th' expectant wee-things,
    toddlin', stacher through
To meet their Dad,
    wi' flichterin' noise and glee.
His wee bit ingle, blinkin' bonilie,
His clean hearth-stane,
    his thrifty wifie's smile,
The lisping infant, prattling at his knee,
Does a' his weary kiaugh and care beguile,
An' makes him quite forget his labour
    an' his toil.

As he approaches his cottage, he is met by his toddlers, who are happy to see their father, and as he sits by his fireside, his toils and tribulations are forgotten in the comfort of his home and his loving wife.
*cot* = cottage; *wee-things* = small children; *stacher* = walk unsteadily; *flichterin'* = fluttering; *ingle* = fireside; *hearth-stane* = hearth-stone; *wifie* = wife; *kiaugh* = trouble

Belyve, the elder bairns come drappin' in,
At service out, amang the farmers roun';
Some ca' the pleugh,
    some herd, some tentie rin
A cannie errand to a neebor town;
Their eldest hope, their Jenny, woman grown,
In youthfu' bloom, love sparkling in her e'e,
Comes hame, perhaps to show
    a braw new gown,
Or deposits her sair-won penny-fee,
To help her parents dear, if they 'n hardship be.

Eventually the older children start arriving home. They have been working for local farmers, or running errands to a nearby town. The eldest daughter, Jenny, is almost a grown woman but she understands the need to help out with the family budget.
*Belyve* = eventually; *bairns* = children; *drappin'* = dropping; *amang* = among; *roun'* = around; *ca' the pleugh* = drive the plough; *tentie rin a cannie errand* = attend to a small errand; *neebor* = neighbour; *e'e* = eye; *braw* = fine; *sair-won penny-fee* = hard-earned small wage

With joy unfeign'd,
    brothers and sisters meet,
And each for other's weelfare kindly spiers:
The social hours, swift-wing'd, unnotic'd fleet;
Each tells the uncos that he sees or hears.
The parents, partial, eye their hopeful years
Anticipation forward points the view,
The mother, wi' her needle an' her sheers,
Gars auld claes look amaist as weel's the new;
The father mixes a' wi' admonition due.

This is a family of true brotherly and sisterly love and affection, and time flies as each recounts the events of the week, while the parents listen and wonder what life has ahead for their offspring. The mother keeps busy with her sewing and repairing, while the father offers words of wisdom.
*weelfare* = welfare; *spiers* = asks; *fleet* = fly by; *uncos* = unusual; *sheers* = scissors; *gars auld claes look amaist as weel's the new* = makes old clothes look almost like new; *a' wi'* = all with

Their master's and their mistress's command,
The younkers a' are warned to obey;
An' mind their labours wi an eydent hand,
An' ne'er tho' ot o' sight to jauk or play;
An' O! be sure to fear the Lord alway!
An' mind your duty, duly, morn an' night;
Lest in temptation's path ye gang astray,
Implore his counsel an' assisting might;
They never sought in vain that
        sought the Lord aright.

Right and wrong are clearly defined
in this family, and the young people
are taught not only to obey their
employers, but, more importantly,
also to follow the word of God at all
times and never be afraid to ask for
His advice.
*younkers* = youngsters; *eydent* =
dilligent; *jauk* = joke; *gang* = go;
*aright* = in the right way

But, hark! A rap comes gently to the door;
Jenny, wha kens the meaning o' the same,
Tells how a neebor lad cam o'er the moor,
To do some errands, and convoy her hame.
The wily mother sees the conscious flame
Sparkle in Jenny's e'e, and flush her cheek;
Wi' heart-struck anxious care,
        inquires his name,
While Jenny, hafflins is afraid to speak;
Weel pleas'd the mother hears, it's nae wild,
        worthless rake.

Here we have a timeless description
of a young suitor arriving to
court the daughter. The daughter's
embarrassment, and the mother's
relief that he is not a ne'er-do-well,
illustrate a situation familiar in
many families.
*rap* = a knock; *wha kens* = who
knows; *cam o'er* = came over;
*hafflins* = half; *weel pleas'd* = well
pleased; *nae* = no; *rake* = waster

Wi' kindly welcome, Jenny brings him ben;
A strappin' youth, he tak's the mother's eye;
Blythe Jenny sees the visit's no ill-ta'en;
The father cracks of horses, pleughs, and kye.
The youngster's artless heart o'erflows wi' joy,
But blate an' laithfu', scarce can weel behave;
The mother, wi' a woman's wiles can spy
What makes the youth sae bashfu' an' sae grave;
Weel pleas'd to think her bairn's
        respected like the lave.

Jenny is relieved to see no
disapproval of the visit. Her mother
obviously likes the lad and father
is happy to discuss farming matters
with him. The lad is bashful and
serious, which pleases the mother,
who recognises that he respects her
daughter.
*ben* = through; *strappin'* = well-built;
*taks* = takes; *no' ill ta'en* = not ill-
taken; *cracks* = talks; *kye* = cattle;
*blate an' laithfu'* = sheepish and
bashful; *the lave* = the others

O happy love! Where love like this is found!
O heart-felt rapture! Bliss beyond compare!
I' ve paced much this weary, mortal round,
And sage experience bids me this declare –
'If Heav'n a draught of heavenly pleasure spare,
One cordial in this melancholy vale,
'Tis when a youthful, loving, modest pair
In other's arms, breathe out the tender tale,
Beneath the milk-white thorn that scents the ev'ning gale.'

At this point, Burns recounts the many times that he himself has experienced the joys of love, and waxes lyrical accordingly.

Is there, in human form, that bears a heart –
A wretch! A villain! Lost to love and truth!
That can, wi' studied, sly ensnaring art,
Betray sweet Jenny's unsuspecting youth?
Curse on his perjur'd arts! dissembling, smooth!
Are honour, virtue, conscience, all exil'd?
Is there no pity, no relenting ruth,
Points to the parents fondling o'er their child?
Then paints the ruin'd maid,
     and their distraction wild?

He goes on to ask how anyone could take advantage of an innocent like Jenny, and curses the wrongdoers for the ruination they bring to entire families. One wonders if the Bard is wearing a hairshirt at this point, and if perhaps these lines are directed at his own far from blameless life. *perjur'd arts* = lies; *dissembling* = masking; *ruth* = remorse

But now the supper crowns their simple board,
The halesome parritch, chief o' Scotia's food;
The soupe their only hawkie does afford,
That 'yont the hallan snugly chows her cood;
The dame brings out in complimental mood,
To grace the lad, her weel-hain'd kebbuck fell,
An' aft he's prest, an' aft he ca's it guid:
The frugal wifie, garrulous will tell
How't was a towmond auld, sin' lint was i' the bell.

Supper consists of porridge, served with milk from their only cow, happily settled behind the partition that separates her from the living quarters, and just to impress a little, the mother produces a cheese that has lain for a year, wrapped in flax. *halesome parritch* = wholesome porridge; *soupe* = milk; *hawkie* = cow; *yont* = beyond; *hallan* = partition; *chows her cood* = chews the cud; *weel-hain'd kebbuck* = a cheese she has saved; *aft* = after; *prest* = pressed; *ca's it good* = calls it good; *towmond auld* = twelve-month old; *sin lint was i' the bell* = since flax was in flower

The cheerfu' supper done, wi' serious face,
They, round the ingle, form a circle wide
The sire turns o'er wi' patriarchial grace,
The big ha'-Bible, ance his father's pride.
His bonnet rev'rently is laid aside,
His lyart haffets wearing thin and bare;
Those strains that once did sweet in Zion glide,
He wales a portion wi' judicious care;
And 'Let us worship God!'
      he says with solemn air.

With supper finished, the family sit around the fireplace. The father removes his hat, revealing thin, greying hair, then brings out the cherished family Bible. He selects a chapter and solemnly tells the family to prepare to worship God. *round the ingle* = round the fireplace; *sire* = father; *ha'-Bible* = family Bible; *ance* = once; *bonnet* = a working man's cap; *lyart haffets* = grey temples; *wales* = selects

They chant their artless notes in simple guise;
They tune their hearts, by far the noblest aim;
Perhaps *Dundee's* wild-warblng measures rise,
Or plaintiff *Martyrs*, worthy o' the name;
Or noble Elgin beets the heavenward flame,
The sweetest far of Scotia's holy lays;
Compar'd with these, Italian trills are tame;
The tickl'd ear no heart-felt raptures raise;
Nae unison hae they, with our Creator's praise.

The family join together in singing a well-known psalm, possibly to one of the traditional Scottish airs mentioned here by the Bard, rather than to one of the joyless Italian tunes which many people favoured. *holy lays* = religious music

The priest-like father reads the sacred page,
How Abram was the friend of God on high;
Or, Moses bade eternal warfare wage
Wi' Amalek's ungracious progeny;
Or, how the royal Bard did groaning lie
Beneath the stroke of Heaven's avenging ire;
Or Job's pathetic plaint, and wailing cry;
Or rapt Isaiah's wild, seraphic fire;
Or other holy Seers that tune the sacred lyre.

Now the father reads the Scriptures in a truly reverent and ministerial fashion, telling the ancient stories from the Bible to his hushed family. *ire* = anger; *plaint* = lamentation; *lyre* = harp

Perhaps the Christian volume is the theme,
How guiltless blood for guilty men was shed;
How He, who bore in Heav'n the second name,
Had not on earth whereon to lay His head;
How His first followers and servants sped;
The precepts sage they wrote to many a land;
How He, who lone in Patmos banished,
Saw in the sun a mighty angel stand,
And heard great Bab'lon's doom
    pronounc'd by Heav'n's command.

Burns now appears to be contemplating the wisdom of the Bible as he writes of the life of Jesus Christ. His knowledge of the Holy Book is impressive as he tells of St John's exile in Patmos, and how he saw the Angel Michael, and heard the order to destroy Babylon, considered by some to be a name describing all heretical religions.

Then kneeling down to Heaven's Eternal King,
The saint, the father, and the husband prays;
Hope 'springs exulting on triumphant wing'
That thus they shall all meet in future days,
There, ever bask in uncreated rays,
No more to sigh, or shed the bitter tear,
Together hymning their Creator's praise,
In such society, yet still more dear;
While circling Time moves round in an
    eternal sphere.

The father exults the praises of the Lord and prays for the day when the family will meet in Heaven, where all cares will be forgotten, and their days will be spent in the praise of the Lord.

Compar'd with this, how poor Religion's pride,
In all the pomp of method, and of art;
When men display to congregations wide
Devotion's ev'ry grace, except the heart!
The Power, incens'd, the pageant will desert,
The pompous strains, the sacerdotal stole;
But, haply, in some cottage far apart,
May hear, well-pleas'd, the language of the soul;
And in His Book of Life the
    inmates poor enrol.

Here again the poet declares his contempt for the pomp and ceremony of the Church, and the lack of heartfelt devotion of many of those who profess to be devout. Their beliefs are hollow when stood against those of the cottagers.
*sacerdotal* = priestly; *haply* = perhaps

Then homeward all take off their sev'ral way;
The youngling cottagers retire to rest;
The parent-pair their secret homage pay,
And proffer up to Heaven the warm request,
That He who stills the raven's clam'rous nest,
And decks the lily fair in flow'ry pride,
Would, in the way His wisdom sees the best,
For them and for their little ones provide;
But, chiefly in their hearts with
    Grace Divine preside.

As the family gathering breaks up and they set off to their various destinations, the parents pray to God that He will provide for all of them, but more importantly, that they will be blessed with His Holy Grace. *youngling* = young; *clam'rous* = clamorous

From scenes like these,
    old Scotia's grandeur springs,
That makes her loved at home, rever'd abroad;
Princes and lords are but the breath of kings,
'An honest man's the noblest work of God;'
And certes in fair Virtue's heavenly road,
The cottage leaves the palace far behind.
What is a lordling's pomp? a cumbrous load,
Disguising oft the wretch of human kind,
Studied in arts of Hell, in wickedness refin'd!

This simplicity of belief is what appears to make Scotland so beloved around the world. Burns does not hesitate to use Alexander Pope's words about their being nothing more noble than an honest man, at the same time pointing out that Lord and Prince are but titles given out by kings. In terms of love and devotion, a cottage is a much worthier place than any palace. *certes* = certainly; *cumbrous* = cumbersome.

O Scotia! My dear, my native soil!
For whom my warmest wish to Heav'n is sent!
Long may thy hardy sons of rustic toil
Be blest with health, and peace,
    and sweet content!
And O! may Heav'n their simple lives prevent
From luxury's contagion, weak and vile!
Then, however crowns and coronets be rent,
A virtuous populace may rise the while,
And stand a wall of fire around
    their much lov'd isle.

Expressing his love for Scotland, the land of his birth, Burns prays that the peace and contentment of its working class will never be ruined by exposure to the luxuries which promote greed and avarice, and that, no matter who wears the crown, the population stand united to protect their beloved country.

O Thou! Who poured the patriotic tide
That streamed thro' Wallace's undaunted heart,
Who dar'd to, nobly, stem tyrannic pride,
Or nobly die, the second glorious part;
(The patriot's God, peculiarly Thou art,
His friend, inspirer, guardian and reward!)
O never, never Scotia's realm desert,
But still the patriot, and the patriot bard,
In bright succession raise,

     her ornament and guard!

Finally he pleads with God, who filled the veins of great Scots such as William Wallace with the patriotic blood which helped fight against the tyrants, that He should never desert the Scots as He is the true God of the patriotic Scottish Nation.

*dar'd* = dared

# Welcome to a Bastart Wean

During the year 1784, the Burns family employed a serving girl named Elizabeth Paton. This young lady became pregnant by Robert Burns, and although it appears that the Bard's mother was quite keen to have the couple married, this did not meet with the approval of his brother and sisters. They apparently considered Elizabeth to be much too rude and uncouth to be a suitable partner for their brother. Burns too must have considered her as being little more than a willing sexual partner, as the poem he wrote about her, My Girl She's Airy, could hardly be considered to be an epistle of love and respect. However, the following lines, dedicated to his illegimate daughter display a true paternal fondness for the child, irrespective of the embarrassment caused by her arrival in the world.

Thou's welcome wean! Mishanter fa' me,
If thoughts o' thee, or yet thy mammie.
Shall ever daunton me or awe me,
My sweet wee lady,
Or if I blush when thou shalt ca' me
Tyta or daddie!

In this opening verse, Burns welcomes the arrival of his child, and asks that misfortune fall upon him should he ever have ill-thoughts about the child or her mother, or if he should be embarrassed when his child calls him Daddy.
wean = child; mishanter = misfortune; fa' = fall; daunton = subdue; awe = owe; shalt ca' = shall call; Tyta = father.

What tho' they ca' me fornicator,
An' tease my name in kintra clatter,
The mair they talk, I'm kend the better,
E'en let them clash!
An auld wife's tongue's a feckless matter
To gie ane fash.

He says that people will call him unkind names and will gossip about him, but that by their talk he will become better known. One should not let gossips worry you.
kintra clatter = talk of the country; mair = more; kend = known; clash = idle talk; auld wife = old woman; feckless = powerless; gie ane fash = give one trouble.

Welcome my bonie, sweet wee dochter!
Tho' ye came here a wee unsought for,
And tho' your coming I hae fought for.
Baith kirk and queir;
Yet, by my faith, ye're no unwrought for –
That I shall swear!

He tells the daughter that even although her arrival was unplanned, she is no less welcome, and that he fought both the church and the courts to ensure her well-being, and that she should never think that she was unwanted. *dochter* = daughter; *wee* = little; *baith* = both; *kirk and queir* = church and court; *unwrought* = unwanted.

Sweet fruit o' monie a merry dint,
My funny toil is no a' tint,
Tho thou cam to the warl' asklent,
Which fools may scoff at,
In my last plack thy part's be in it
The better half o't.

Athough the result of many a happy liaison between her parents, some people may mock her for being illegitimate, but that he will spend his last penny to ensure her well-being. *monie* = many; *dint* = liaison; *a' tint* = all lost; *warl* = world; *asklent* = obliquely; *plack* = small coin; *o't* = of it

Tho' I should be the waur bestead,
Thou's be as braw and bienly clad,
And thy young years as nicely bred,
Wi' education,
As onie brat o' wedlock's bed,
In a' thy station.

Although it will make him poorer, he will see that she is as well-dressed, well brought up, and well-educated as any child born to married parents. *waur* = worse; *bestead* = position; *braw* = beautifu; *bienly* = comfortably; *onie brat o' wedlock's bed* = legitimate child

Wee image o' my bonie Betty,
As fatherly I kiss and daut thee,
As dear, and near my heart I set thee
Wi' as guid will,
As a' the priests had seen me get thee
That's out o' Hell.

Gude grant that thou may ay inherit
Thy mither's looks an' gracefu' merit,
An' thy poor worthless daddie's spirit,
Without his failin's!
'Twill please me mair to see thee heir it,
Than stockit mailins.

And if thou be what I wad hae thee,
An' tak the counsel I shall gie thee,
I'll never rue my trouble wi' thee –
The cost nor shame o't –
But be a loving father to thee,
And brag the name o't.

He sees in her a miniature of her lovely mother, and as he kisses her, he promises to love and cherish her, despite the terrible disapproval of the church.
*daut* = pet

He asks that God grants her her mother's beauty and graceful demeanour, and that she be given his spirit but without his faults. She will be better off with these gifts than having a well-stocked farm.
*Gude* = God; *ay* = always; *mither* = mother; *heir* = inherit; *stockit mailins* = well-stocked farm

Finally he tells her that if she takes his advice and grows up as he would wish, then he will never regret the shame that he brought on himself, but that he will be a truly loving father who boasts about his child.

# The Twa Dogs

A TALE OF THOSE WHO HAVE, AND THOSE WHO HAVE NOT,
THE QUESTION IS, WHICH GROUP IS WHICH?

Burns had a dog named Luath that he loved dearly. Sadly, Luath came to an untimely end and the poet resolved to immortalise his old and trusted friend by writing this very fine story. Luath represents the working people of Scotland, while Caesar, a name conjured up by the poet, represents the ruling classes.

Perhaps this poem suggests a reason why the works of Burns are so popular in the Soviet Union.

'Twas in that place o' Scotland's Isle.
That bears the name o' auld King Coil,
Upon a bonie day in June
When wearin thro' the afternoon,
Twa dogs, that were na thrang at hame,
For'gather'd ance upon a time.

One fine day in June, at Kyle in Scotland, two very dissimiliar dogs who had nothing to do at home, met up with each other.
*King Coil* = a Pictish monarch; *thro'* = through; *twa* = two; *na thrang at hame* = not busy at home; *for'gather'd* = met; *ance* = once

The first I'll name, they ca'd him Caesar,
Was keepit for 'his Honour's' pleasure,
His hair, his size, his mouth, his lugs,
Shew'd he was nane o' Scotland's dogs;
But whalpit some place far abroad,
Whare sailors gang to fish for cod.

The first was named Caesar, and was purely a pet for his master. His size and shape indicated that he was not native to Scotland, but had probably come from Newfoundland.
*ca'd* = called; *keepit* = kept; *lugs* = ears; *shew'd* = showed; *nane* = none; *whalpit* = born; *whare* = where; *gang* = go

His locked, letter'd, braw brass collar
Shew'd him the gentleman an' scholar;
But tho' he was o' high degree,
The fient a pride, nae pride had he;
But wad hae spent an hour caressin',
Ev'n wi' a tinkler-gipsy's messin;
At kirk or market, mill or smiddie,
Nae tawted tyke, tho' e'er sae duddie,
But he wad stan't, as glad to see him,
An' stroant on stanes an' hillocks wi' him.

Despite his fancy collar and high
pedigree, he was totally without
ambition and was willing to spend
his days with any old mongrel
willing to spend time with him.
*braw* = handsome; *The fient a* = a bit
of the devil; *nae* = no, *wad hae* =
would have; *messin* = mongrel;
*kirk* = church; *smiddy* = smith;
*nae tauted tyke* = no matted dog;
*e'er sae duddie* = ever so ragged;
*wad stan't* = would stand; *stroant
on stanes* = pissed on stones

The tither was a ploughman's collie,
A rhyming, ranting, raving billie,
Wha for his friend an' comrade had him,
And in his freaks had Luath ca'd him.
After some dog in Highland sang,
Was made lang syne – Lord knows how lang.

The other was a collie named
Luath, owned by a poetic
ploughman, and obviously based on
Burns' dog of the same name.
*tither* = other; *ranting* = joyous;
*billie* = comrade; *in his freaks* =
in amusement; *lang syne* = long ago

He was a gash an' faithfu' tyke,
As ever lap a sheugh or dyke,
His honest, sonsie, baws'nt face
Ay gat him friends in ilka place;
His breast was white, his tousie back
Weel clad wi' coat o' glossy black;
His gawsie tail wi' upward curl,
Hung owre his hurdies wi' a swirl.

He was as respectable and faithful
a dog as had ever leapt over
ditches and walls, and with his
friendly face with its white stripe,
and his happily wagging tail, he was
guaranteed a welcome anywhere.
*gash* = wise; *lap* = leapt; *sheugh* =
ditch; *dyke* = stone wall; *sonsie* =
jolly; *bawsn't* = white-striped; *gat* =
got; *ilka* = every; *tousie* = shaggy;
*weel* = well; *gawsie* =handsome;
*owre his hurdies* = over his backside

Nae doubt but that they were fain o' ither,
An' unco pack an' thick thegither;
Wi' social noses whyles snuff'd an' snowkit;
Whyles mice an' muddie worts they howkit;
Whyles scour'd awa; in lang excursion,
An' worry'd ither in diversion;
'Till tired at last wi' monie a farce,
They set them down upon their arse,
An' there began a lang digression
About the 'lords o' the creation'

There was no doubt that these two dogs enjoyed each other's company as they sniffed out mice and moles and went for long walks. Eventually however, they would tire of playing and settle down for serious discussion about the meaning of life.
*fain o' ither;* = fond of each other; *pack an' thick thegither* = on friendly terms; *whyles* = sometimes; *snuff' an' snowkit* = sniffed and snuffled; *muddieworts* = moles; *howkit* = dug up; *scour'd* = rushed; *monie a farce* = many a laugh

## CAESAR

I've often wonder'd, honest Luath,
What sort o' life poor dogs like you have;
An' when the gentry's life I saw,
What way poor bodies liv'd ava.

Caesar expresses his wonder at he different lifestyles of the rich and the poor.
*ava* = at all

Our laird gets in his racked rents,
His coals, his kain, an' a' his stents;
He rises when he likes himsel';
His flunkies answer at the bell;
He ca's his coach, he ca's his horse;
He draws a bonie silken purse,
As lang's my tail, whare thro' the steeks,
The yellow-letter'd Geordie keeks.

Our master gets his money by charging exorbitant rents. His fuel, his food and his taxes are provided by his tenants. His servants rush to get him his coach or his horse. One can see the golden guineas shining through the stitches of his purse.
*racked* = exorbitant; *kain* = farm produce paid as rent; *stents* = taxes; *flunkies* = servants; *ca's* = calls; *steeks* = stitches; *yellow-letter'd Geordie* = a guinea; *keeks* = peeps

Frae morn to e'en it's nought but toiling,
At baking, roasting, frying, boiling;
An' tho' the gentry first are stechin,
Yet ev'n the ha' folk fill their pechan
Wi' sauce, ragouts, an' sic like trashtrie
That's little short o' downright wastrie.
Our whipper-in, wee blastit wonner,
Poor, worthless elf, it eats a dinner,
Better than onie tenant-man
His Honour has in a' the lan';
An' what poor cot-folk pit their painch in,
I own it's past my comprehension.

Food is prepared all day long. The masters are the first to be served, but the servants get their share – the miserable little kennelman eats better than any of his lordships tenants. I really don't know what the cottagers get to fill their stomach.

*stechin* = completely full; *ha' folk* = house servants; *pechan* = stomach; *sic* = such; *trashtrie* = rubbish; *wastrie* = extravagance; *whipper-in* = kennelman; *wee blastit wonner* = worthless person; *cot-folk* = cottagers; *pit* = put; *painch* = stomach

LUATH

Trowth, Caesar, whyles they're fash't eneugh;
A cotter howkin' in a sheugh,
Wi' dirty stanes biggin' a dyke,
Bearing a quarry, an sic like.
Himsel', a wife he thus sustains,
A smytrie o' wee duddie weans,
An' nought but his han' darg to keep
Them right an' tight in thack an' rape.

Oh, they are worried at times, but they work hard to earn enough to keep a roof over their heads.

*trowth* = truth; *fash't eneugh* = troubled enough; *cotter* = labourer; *biggin'* = building; *smytrie o' wee duddie bairns* = family of small, ragged children; *han' darg* = hands work; *in thack an' rape* = with a roof over their heads

An' when they meet wi' sair disasters,
Like loss o' health or want o' masters,
Ye maist wad think, a wee touch langer,
An' they maun starve o' cauld and hunger;
But how it comes, I never kend yet,
They're maistly wonderfu' contented;
An' buirdly chiels, an' clever hizzies,
Are bred in sic a way as this is.

When problems arise like ill-health or unemployment, you would expect them to die of cold and hunger. I don't know how they survive, but they usually appear contented, and they manage to raise sturdy boys and clever girls.

*sair* = sore; *ye maist wad think* = you would believe; *a wee touch langer* = a little longer; *maun* = must; *cauld* = cold; *kend* = knew; *maistly* = mostl; *buirdly chiels* = sturdy lads; *hizzies* = young women

## CAESAR

But then to see how you're negleckit,
How huff'd, an' cuff'd, an' disrespeckit!
Lord man, our gentry care as little
For delvers, ditchers, an' sic cattle;
They gang as saucy by poor folk,
As I wad by a stinking brock.

But no one respects either you or the cottagers. The gentry pass you as I would pass a stinking old badger.

*negleckit* = neglected; *huff'd* = bullied; *cuff'd* = beaten; *ditchers* = ditch-cleaners; *sic cattle* = such people; *wad* = would; *brock* = badger

I've notic'd, on our laird's court-day,
(An' monie a time my heart's been wae),
Poor tenant bodies, scant o' cash,
How they maun thole a factor's snash;
He'll stamp an' threaten, curse an' swear,
He'll apprehend them, poind their gear;
While they maun stan', wi aspect humble,
An' hear it a', an' fear an' tremble!
I see how folk live that hae riches;
But surely poor-folk maun be wretches!

I've been sore-hearted many times
on rent days by the way the
landlord's agent abuses tenants who
cannot pay their dues. He threatens
and curses them and has them
arrested, and he impounds their
few possessions while all they can
do is stand and tremble. I can see
how the rich live, but being poor
must be terrible.

*scant o' cash* = short of money;
*maun thole* = must endure; *factor's
snash* = abuse from the agent; *poind*
= seize

## LUATH

They're no sae wretched 's ane wad think;
Tho' constantly on poortith's brink,
They're sae accustom'd wi' the sight,
The view o't gies them little fright.

They are so used to being close to
poverty that they hardly notice it,
and it does not worry them
unduly.

*poortith's brink* = edge of poverty

Then chance and fortune are sae guided,
They're ay in less or mair provided,
An' tho' fatigued wi' close employment,
A blink o' rest's a sweet enjoyment.

They have little control of their
own destiny, and as they are
constantly exhausted, a little nap is
a great treat to them.

*blink o' rest* = a short nap

The dearest comfort o' their lives,
Their gushie weans an' faithfu' wives;
The prattlin' things are just the pride,
That sweetens a' their fireside.

Their greatest pleasure is simply to
be at home with their family.
*gushie weans* = thriving children;
*prattlin'* = chattering.

An' whyles twalpennie worth o' nappy
Can mak their bodies unco happy;
They lay aside their private cares,
To mind the Kirk and State affairs;
They'll talk o' patronage an' priests,
Wi' kindlin' fury in their breasts,
Or tell what new taxation's comin',
An' ferlie at the folk in Lon'on.

While the ale does help them relax,
they are serious-minded people
who discuss in depth the affairs of
Church and State. Talking of
patronage and priesthood can
stir them to anger and they discuss
with amazement these people in
London who burden them with
yet more taxes.
*twalpenny worth o' nappy* =
twelvepence worth of ale;
*wi' kindlin' fury* = with burning
passion; *ferlie* = marvel

As bleak-fac'd Hallowmass returns,
They get the jovial, ranting kirns,
When rural life of ev'ry station,
Unite in common recreation;
Love blinks, Wit slaps, an' social Mirth
Forgets there's Care upo' the earth.

When the harvest is in and they
are into autumn, they have the
most wonderful parties where you
would scarce believe that they
had a care in the world.
*rantin' kirns* = harvest festivals

That merry day the year begins,
They bar the door on frosty win's;
The nappy reeks wi' mantle ream,
An' sheds a heart-inspiring stream,
The luntin' pipe an' sneeshin' mill,
Are handed round wi' right guid-will;
The cantie auld folks crackin' crouse,
The young anes rantin' thro' the house–
My heart has been sae fain to see them,
That I for joy hae barkit wi' them.

The arrival of a New Year heralds
another happy time when the
ale flows freely and pipes and snuff
are handed around. The elders
enjoy a good talk, and the children
play so happily that I bark with joy
just to be there with them.
*win's* = winds; *the nappy reeks wi'
mantling ream* = the room
smells of foaming al; *luntin'* =
smoking; *sneeshin' mill* =
snuff box; *cantie auld folks crackin'
crouse* = cheerful old folk
talking merrily; *sae fain* = so glad;
*hae barkit* = have barked.

Still it's owre true that ye hae said,
Sic game is now owre aften play'd;
There' monie a creditable stock
O decent, honest, fawsont folk,
Are riven out baith root an' branch,
Some rascal's pridefu' greed to quench,
Wha thinks to knit himsel' the faster
In favour wi' some gentle master,
Wha aiblins, thrang a parliamentin',
For Britain's guid his soul indentin' –

Nevertheless, there's a lot of truth in what you have said. Many's the family that's been forced out of their home by some unscrupulous agent trying to win favour with his master who is busy with affairs of the state.

*fawsont* = dignified; *riven* = torn; *baith* = both; *gentle* = gentleman; *aiblins thrang a parliamentin'* = perhaps busy in parliament; *his saul indentin* = giving his soul

## CAESAR

Haith, lad ye ken little about it;
For Britain's guid! guid faith I doubt it.
Say, rather, gaun as Premiers lead him;
An' saying aye, or no's they bid him;
At operas an' plays parading,
Mortgaging, gambling, masquerading;
Or maybe in a frolic daft,
To Hague or Calais taks a waft,
To mak a tour an' tak a whirl,
To learn bon-ton, an' see the worl'.

Huh, lad, you do not know the half of it. Working for Britain's good? No, they simply do what their party leaders tell them. Most of the time they're going to the opera or to plays, or they are gambling or going to fancy-dress balls. Or they they might decide to go to The Hague or Calais, or even further afield on the Grand Tour.

*ye little ken* = you little know; *gaun* = going; *taks a waft* = take a trip.

There, at Vienna or Versailles,
He rives his father's auld entails;
Or by Madrid he takes the rout,
To thrum guitars an' fecht wi' nowt;
Or down Italian vista startles,
Whore-hunting amang groves o' myrtles;
Then bowses drumlie German-water,
To mak himsel' look fair an' fatter,
An' clear the consequential sorrows,
Love-gifts of Carnival signoras,
For Britain's guid! For her destruction!
Wi' dissipation, feud an' faction.

They will spend their father's
money in Vienna or Versailles, or
perhaps in Madrid where they
listen to the music and watch the
bull-fights, or go womanizing in
Italy before they finish up in some
German spa where they drink the
muddy mineral water in order to
try to improve their appearance
and hopefully, to clear up the sexual
disease picked up from some
foreign girl. Forget about them
working for Britain's good! They
are destroying her with their
dissipation and self-indulgence!
*rives his auld father's entails* = wastes
his inheritance; *thrum* = strum;
*fecht wi' nowt* = fight bulls; *bowses
drumlie German-water* = drinks
muddy German mineral waters

## LUATH

Hech man! dear sirs! Is that the gate
They waste sae monie a braw estate!
Are we sae foughten an' harass'd
For gear to gang that gate at last?

We work hard for them while they
waste it all away.
*gate* = way, *sae monie a braw estate* =
many a fine inheritance; *foughten* =
troubled

O would they stay aback frae courts,
An' please themsels wi' countra sports,
It wad for ev'ry ane be better.
The laird, the tenant, and the cotter!
For thae frank, rantin', ramblin' billies,
Fient haet o' them 's ill-hearted fellows;
Except for breakin' o' their timmer,
Or speakin' lightly o' their limmer,
Or shootin' of a hare or moor-cock,
The ne'er a bit they're ill to poor folk.

Why can't they just stay at home
and enjoy country pursuits.
Everyone would be much better off.
They are really not such bad
fellows you know, although
their manners are often poor in
the way they discuss their affairs
with women so openly, or go
shooting hare or moorhens just for
the fun of it. They are certainly
never nasty to us poor folk.
*countra* = country; *fient haet* = not
one of; *timmer* = timber; *limmer* =
mistress

But will ye tell me master Caesar,
Sure great folks' life's a life o' pleasure?`
Nae cauld nor hunger e'er can steer them,
The vera thought o't need na fear them.

But surely Caesar, their life is one
of pure pleasure? No worries at all
of cold and hunger to upset them.
*vera* = very

CAESAR

Lord man, were ye but whyles whare I am,
The gentles ye wad ne'er envy 'em!

If you knew what I knew, you
would not envy them.

It's true they need na starve or sweat,
Thro' winter's cauld, or simmer's heat;
They've nae sair wark to craze their banes,
An' fill auld age wi' grips an' granes;
But human bodies are sic fools,
For a' their colleges an' schools,
That when nae real ills perplex them,
They mak enow themselves to vex them;
An' aye the less they hae to sturt them,
In like proportion, less will hurt them.

It is true that they neither starve
nor sweat, and their bodies are
not racked with the pain of toil, but
humans are strange creatures and
in spite of their education, if they
have no real ills to trouble them,
then they will find something to
make them ill for little or no
reason.
*simmer* = summer; *sair work* =
sore work; *to craze their banes* = to
injure their bones; *wi grips an'
granes* = with aches and groans;
*enow* = enough; *sturt* = trouble.

A countra fellow at the pleugh,
His acre's till'd, he's right eneugh;
A countra girl at her wheel,
Her dizzen's dune, she's unco weel;
But gentlemen, an' ladies warst,
Wi' ev'n down want o' wark are curst
They loiter, lounging, lank an' lazy;
Tho' deil haet ails them, yet uneasy:
Their days insipid, dull an' tasteless;
Their nights unquiet, lang an' restless.

When country workers have
completed their tasks, they get a
feeling of personal satisfaction. But
the gentlemen, and even worse – the
ladies – have nothing to do but pass
the time, lounging around and
becoming bored. Their days are long
and tedious, and their nights are
just as bad.
*dizzen's dune* = dozen's done;
*unco weel* = very well

An' ev'n their sports, their balls an' races,
Their galloping thro' public places,
There's sic parade, sic pomp an' art,
The joy can scarcely reach the heart.

They find little joy in their sports
and balls, or at the race meetings,
just making sure that they are seen
in all the right places.

The men cast out in party-matches,
Then sowther a' in deep debauches;
Ae night they're mad wi' drink or whoring,
Niest day their life is past enduring.

The men get drunk, and throw
their money away on prostitutes
and gambling, and wake next day
with massive hangovers.
*party-matches* = groups;
*sowther* = make up; *deep debauches* =
heavy drinking; *niest* = next

The ladies arm-in-arm in clusters.
As great an' gracious as their sisters;
But hear their absent thoughts o' ither
They're a' run deils an' jads thegither,
Whyles owre the wee bit cup an' platie,
They sip the scandal-potion pretty;
Or lee-lang nights, wi' crabbit leuks
Pore owre the devil's pictur'd beuks;
Stake on a chance a farmer's stackyard,
An' cheat like onie unhang'd blackguard.

The women act so sisterly and
gracious while they sip their tea
and seek the latest scandal about
their friends. Or they sit, scowling,
while they play cards, gambling
with their tenants' livelihood, and
cheating shamelessly.
*jad* = ill-tempered woman;
*platie* = plate; *crabbit leuks* =
sour-faced; *devil's pictur'd beuks* =
playing cards; *stackyard* = stockyard

There's some exceptions, man an' woman;
But this is Gentry's life in common.

There are a few exceptions, but not
many.

By this time the sun was out o' sight,
An' darker gloamin' brought the night;
The bum-clock humm'd wi' lazy drone;
The kye stood rowtin' i' the loan;
When up they gat an' shook their lugs,
Rejoic'd they were na men but dogs,
An' each took aff his several way,
Resolv'd to meet some ither day.

By now darkness was falling.
Beetles were droning in the
twilight, and the cattle were lowing
in the fields. The two dogs arose,
shook themselves and considered
how fortunate they were to be
dogs and not men. Then each went
his own way vowing to meet again.
*gloamin'* = twilight; *bum-clock* =
drone-beetle; *kye* = cattle;
*lugs* = ears.

# The Lass O' Ballochmyle

Burns set eyes upon this young lady while out for an evening stroll, and being the great romantic, was so excited by her beauty that he composed the following verses in her honour. In an attempt to ingratiate himself with the lass, Wilhelmina Alexander, he wrote to her, enclosing the poem in the obvious hope that they might form some sort of relationship. However, Wilhelmina was not prepared tp play the poet's game. Possibly she was aware of his reputation, and she chose to ignore Burns' advances. Surprisingly for one of her beauty, she never did marry, but kept the poet's tribute throughout her life. Once again, and in common with most of Burns' romantic works, the verses speak clearly for themselves and require no further explanation.

'Twas even – the dewy fields were green,
On every blade the pearls hang;
The zephyr wanton'd round the bean,
And bore its fragrant sweets alang;
In every glen the mavis sang,
All nature list'ning seem'd the while,
Except where greenwood echoes rang
Among the braes o' Ballochmyle


With careless step I onward stray'd,
My heart rejoic'd in nature's joy,
When, musing in a lonely glade,
A maiden fair I chanc'd to spy;
Her look was like the morning's eye,
Her air like nature's vernal smile;
Perfection whisper'd, passing by,
'Behold the lass o' Ballochmyle!'

Fair is the morn in flow'ry May
And sweet is night in autumn mild;
When roving thro' the garden gay,
Or wand'ring in a lonely wild;
But Woman, Nature's darling child!
There all her charms she does compile;
Ev'n there her other works are foil'd
By the bonie lass o' Ballochmyle.


O had she been a country maid,
And I the happy country swain,
Tho' shelter'd in the lowest shed
That ever rose on Scotland's plain!
Thro' weary winter's wind and rain,
With joy, with rapture I would toil;
And nightly to my bosom strain
The bonie lass o' Ballochmyle


Then pride might climb the slipp'ry steep,
Where fame and honours lofty shine;
And thirst of gold might tempt the deep,
Or downward seek the Indian mine;
Give me the cot below the pine,
To tend the flocks or till the soil;
And every day have joys divine
With the bonie lass o' Ballochmyle.

# Scots Prologue for Mrs Sutherland

ON HER BENEFIT AT THE THEATRE, DUMFRIES, MARCH 3RD, 1790

Burns became involved with a new theatre being built in Dumfries around 1790, and he wrote the following lines to the wife of the proprietor. His irritation at the lack of Scottish material for theatre-goers is evident.

What needs this din about the town o' Lon'on,
How this new play an' that new song is comin'?
Why is outlandish stuff sae meikle courted?
Does Nonsense mend like brandy –
    when imported?
Is there nae poet, burning keen for fame,
Will bauldly try to gie us plays at hame?
For comedy abroad he need na toil,
A knave and fool are plants of every soil.
Nor need to hunt as far as Rome or Greece
To gather matter for the serious piece;
There's themes enow in Caledonian story
Would show the tragic Muse in a' her glory.

In the opinion of Burns, there is little merit in London's influence upon the arts in Scotland. Rubbish will always be rubbish. Surely there is a writer who can recognise that it is unnecessary to look beyond the history of Scotland to find enough material for a serious drama to equal any Greek or Roman tragedy.

*din* = noise; *sang* = song; *sae meikle* = so greatly; *mend* = improve; *bauldly* = boldly; *enow* = enough

Is there no daring Bard will rise and tell
How glorious Wallace stood, how hapless fell?
Where are the Muses fled that could produce
A drama worthy o' the name o' Bruce?
How here, even here, he first unsheath'd the sword
'Gainst mighty England and her guilty lord,
And after monie a bloody, deathless doing,
Wrench'd his dear country from the
    jaws of Ruin!
O, for a Shakespeare, or an Otway scene
To paint the lovely, hapless Scottish Queen!

Is there not a writer who can describe the struggles and dreadful death that claimed William Wallace; are there no playwrights who can tell of Bruce's great battles against the English tyrant? Oh, for a Scottish Shakespeare who would write of the tribulations which befell Mary Queen of Scots.

*Otway* = a 17th-century dramatist

Vain all th' omnipotence of female charms
'Gainst headlong, ruthless, mad
    Rebellion' arms.
She fell, but fell with spirit truly Roman.
To glut the vengeance of a rival woman;
A woman (tho' the phrase may seem uncivil),
As able – and as cruel – as the Devil!
One Douglas lives in Home's immortal page,
But Douglasses were heroes every age:
And tho' your fathers, prodigal of life,
A Douglas followed to the marital strife,
Perhaps, if bowls row right, the Right succeeds,
Ye may yet follow where a Douglas leads!

Mary was the victim of the evil and jealous Elizabeth the First of England, and was condemned to be beheaded by this woman whose cruelty could equal that of the Devil himself. Although the Douglasses have fought for generations on the side of freedom for Scotland, only one is immortalised in print, yet the opportunity may yet arise to follow a Douglas in the battle for freedom. *glut* = satiate; *Home* = Earls of Home, an old border family; *row* = roll

As ye have generous done, if a' the land
Would take the Muses servants by the hand;
Not only hear, but patronise, befriend them,
And where ye justly can commend,
    commend them;
And aiblins, when they winna stand the test,
Wink hard, and say:
    'The folks hae done their best!'
Would a' the land do this, then I'll be caition,
Ye'll soon hae poets o' the Scottish nation
Will gar Fame blaw until her trumpet crack,
And warsle Time, an' lay him on his back!

If only others would follow the example of Mrs Sutherland and encourage writers through patronage, friendship and understanding that not all will attain perfection, then so many poets and writers will emerge from Scotland that the trumpet of fame will blow until it breaks. *aiblins* = perhaps; *caition* = guarantee; *gar* = make; *warsle* = wrestle

For us and for our stage, should onie spier,
'Whase aught the chiels maks a' this bustle here?'
My best leg foremost, I'll set up my brow,
We have the honour to belong to you!
We're a' your ain bairns, e'en guide us as ye like,
But like good mothers, shore before you strike;
And gratefu' still, I trust ye'll ever find us,
For gen'rous patronage, and meikle kindness
We've got frae a' professions, setts an' ranks;
God help us! We're but poor
   – ye'se get but thanks!

Should anyone ask who are we
fellows creating such a stir upon
the stage, Burns will bow and say
that we are your children, to be
guided by you. But if we are to be
criticised, then do it gently. You will
find us ever grateful for your
patronage, but as we have no
money, can only repay you
with our grateful thanks.

*spier* = ask; *whase aught thae chiels
maks a' this bustle here* = who owns
these people making all this activity
here; *shore* = threaten; *meikle* = great;
*setts* = groups

# I Love My Jean

In this eloquent tribute to his new bride, Jean Armour, the Bard expresses his joy and delight at being with her, and explains how the beauties of nature constantly bring her to mind.

O' a' the airts the wind can blaw      *airts* = directions; *blaw* = blow
I dearly love the west,
For there the bonie lassie lives,
The lassie I lo'e best;
There wild-woods grow, and rivers row      *row* = roll
And monie a hill between;
But day and night my fancy's flight
Is ever wi' my Jean.


I see her in the dewy flowers,
I see her sweet and fair;
I hear her in the tunefu' birds,
I hear her charm the air;
There's not a bonie flower that springs
By fountain, shaw or green;      *shaw* = wooded dell
There's not a bonie bird that sings,
But minds me o' my Jean.

# On Marriage

In sharp contrast to the words relating his love for his new bride, these few short lines on marriage would appear to demonstrate Burns' inability to dedicate his life to any one of his many loves, and indeed, show just how bored he became with married life.

That hackney'd judge of human life,
The Preacher and the King,
Observes: 'The man that gets a wife,
He gets a noble thing.'

*That hackney'd judge* = King Solomon

But how capricious are mankind,
Now loathing, now desirous!
We married men, how oft we find
The best of things will tire us!